T0149661

COSMIC ASCENSION PATHWAYS

Key Prayers for Cosmic Ascension

AMERISSIS KUMARA

BALBOA
PRESS

A DIVISION OF HAY HOUSE

Copyright © 2018 Amerissis Kumara.

All rights reserved. No part of this book may be used or reproduced by any means, graphic, electronic, or mechanical, including photocopying, recording, taping or by any information storage retrieval system without the written permission of the author except in the case of brief quotations embodied in critical articles and reviews.

Balboa Press books may be ordered through booksellers or by contacting:

Balboa Press
A Division of Hay House
1663 Liberty Drive
Bloomington, IN 47403
www.balboapress.com.au
1 (877) 407-4847

Because of the dynamic nature of the Internet, any web addresses or links contained in this book may have changed since publication and may no longer be valid. The views expressed in this work are solely those of the author and do not necessarily reflect the views of the publisher, and the publisher hereby disclaims any responsibility for them.

The author of this book does not dispense medical advice or prescribe the use of any technique as a form of treatment for physical, emotional, or medical problems without the advice of a physician, either directly or indirectly. The intent of the author is only to offer information of a general nature to help you in your quest for emotional and spiritual well-being. In the event you use any of the information in this book for yourself, which is your constitutional right, the author and the publisher assume no responsibility for your actions.

Any people depicted in stock imagery provided by Getty Images are models, and such images are being used for illustrative purposes only.
Certain stock imagery © Getty Images.

Print information available on the last page.

ISBN: 978-1-5043-1273-8 (sc)
ISBN: 978-1-5043-1274-5 (e)

Balboa Press rev. date: 03/28/2018

Dedication

I dedicate this Prayer book to all the Lightworkers of Planet Earth and throughout the Universe, who are in Service to the All That Is, The One, the Ultimate and Supreme God of All Creations.

I Acknowledge the Planetary Hierarchy:
The Planetary Logos: Lord Gautama Buddha.
Lord Sanat Kumara and Lady Venus,
Planetary Christ: Lord Maitreya.
Universal Logos: Lord Melchizedek.
The Great Divine Director: Master Ragoczy.
The Maha Chohan: Master St. Germain and the Chohans of the Twelve Sacred Flames and Rays of Christed Light Consciousness.
The Universal Judge:
The Masters and Lady Masters of Love and Light:
All the Archangels, their Divine Complements and
the Legions of Angels who serve the Sacred Flames and Rays:

I pay tribute to them for their great truth, wisdom, unconditional love, compassion, understanding, purification, mercy, dedication and perseverance. For in keeping the Sacred Flames and Rays of Christed Light of God Consciousness alive, they have been and are instrumental in saving Humanity and Planet Earth, (our Glorious and Precious Mother).

I AM in Gratitude from the very depths of the Sacred Chambers of My Heart for their Service to Humanity, Planet Earth and All the Kingdoms and Realms of Planet Earth.

I especially wish to acknowledge, Master Adama, High Priest of Telos, and the Council of Elders of Telos, for bringing the teachings of Lemuria to Humanity through the beloved channel and medium, Aurelia

Louise Jones. I Thank Aurelia for the Blessing of Her Life and dedication to bringing the teachings of Master Adama of Telos and the Heart of Lemuria, and the Masters and Lady Masters of the Seven Sacred Flames to the Conscious Awareness of Humanity.

I acknowledge The One, the Ultimate and Supreme God of All Creations and my Mighty I AM Presence, for the precious words of Christed Light of God Consciousness that are within the Prayers. These channelled words from the Light Realm have become the voice of the Key Prayers for Cosmic Ascension contained within the teachings of this book.

Blessings to You,
Amerissis Kumara

Contents

The Purpose of This Book

The Purpose of this Prayer Book is to inform and assist you on your pathway to Healing and Ascension, through the frequency and vibration of the Prayers, Affirmations and Healing processes. They are designed to access your inner belief systems and bring to your conscious awareness - from your cellular memory and unconscious and subconscious mind - the negative mental and emotional beliefs, patterns and programs that are affecting your life in detrimental ways.

This Book is called –

Cosmic Ascension Pathways Key Prayers for Cosmic Ascension

The Prayers contain Affirmations which are Keys, in that they are stated in the positive. This is so that the lower mind, the ego, will respond with negative thoughts or feelings. From this you will gain insights into what beliefs, patterns and programs you have running from your unconscious mind.

The Prayers are the Keys that will help you open the doorways to access your hidden unconscious memories. The affirmations within each Prayer are Keys that will bring forth beliefs that show the reverse of the affirmation.

The Sacred Flames and Rays each have Key attributes that they enhance and amplify on certain days of the week. Also, if you have an issue or problem with a particular Sacred Flame or Ray attribute, the energy and vibration of the Sacred Flame of that Ray will help you heal the issue or problem, and reframe to a positive outcome by your having received consciously its Wisdom and Understanding.

The information about the day in which each of the Rays is amplified on is found on the Cover for each of the Sacred Flames and Rays/

Foreword

The Prayers for the Twelve Sacred Flames and Rays are <u>powerful</u>, and are designed to help you to Access your Unconscious Mind. They are <u>not</u> comfort prayers, or prayers to create energy, but prayers that help you gain Access to the Energy created by the hidden beliefs within you, which prevent you from seeing beyond the Veils, to the Truth of who you really are, thus clearing away the illusions, so that you are able to be the in reality.

<u>The Prayers can be used in many ways:</u>

<u>Prayers for Ascension</u>

These help you see beyond the Veils of Forgetfulness to the Truth, by having cleared from the Unconscious Mind, the beliefs, patterns and programs that have kept you tied to the cycles of reincarnation.

<u>Prayers to Heal in One's lifetime the</u>
<u>Causes of what you are at the Effects of</u>

The Prayers help you eliminate the causes through the healing gained from the Sacred Flames and Rays, coupled with the releasing, relinquishing and handing over of old negative beliefs, to your Mighty I Am Presence or the Sacred Flames and Rays of Christed Light of God Consciousness, thus changing the negative causes to positive causes.

The transformation of the old negative belief patterns to new positive belief patterns is very important for your inner growth and Ascension to Ever - Higher Levels of Consciousness. This will happen once you have the Wisdom and Understanding of your old negative beliefs, and changed them into positive ones.

Prayers to the Twelve Sacred Flames and Rays

These are able to cancel out negative energy and bring in positive energy to all areas of the Mind, Body and Physical Heart. The Positive Energy of the Sacred Flames and Rays remove the Negative Energy, eliminating it from your Mind, Body and Physical Heart. The Sacred Heart, which your Divine-Self, (True-Self) resides, is All Knowing, Eternally Free, Forgiving and Unconditional Love, because your True-Self is the God-Self within.

Prayers for Enlightenment

Held within these prayers are many Wisdoms, Understandings and Information coming to you from the Ascended Masters, and the Sacred Flames and Rays of Christed Light Consciousness.

Prayers for Healing

There are special healing prayers in this book that are meant to be used for Self-Healing, both in private and group situations. These prayers are **processing prayers**. When you work with them, feel the energy of your Divine-Self within you and working through you. If you cannot feel the energy, trust that the process in happening. Know; that the more you trust, the more likely it is that you will begin to feel the energy.

There can be resistance to the Prayers coming from one's Ego, (False Self).

For your continued Healing and Growth, you are to research any thoughts and feeling of resistance within yourself, these can be blocks caused and created and by the Ego, they stem from egoism, arrogance and control of you (the person), in an effort to prevent your evolution and growth to enlightenment, self-awareness and healing.

Nothing is outside of self, all is within you. Because the energy of the Universe is all in Oneness, there is always energy. If you are unable to feel that energy or even be aware of it, then something within yourself is blocking you from feeling, knowing and accessing the energy that emanates from the Divine True-Self and the Universe around you. You need to be aware of the many avenues that the Ego is prepared to use in its efforts to be in control and prevent you from being your True-Self and connected to the Universal Mind of God, which is The One, the Ultimate and Supreme God of All Creations, the All That Is.

Prayers for Shifting Consciousness

These Prayers can help you shift to higher levels of Consciousness. This happens when a person reads and studies the Prayers silently. And then ponders the messages contained within the prayers. You can select paragraphs, phrases and words from the Prayers that resonate for you as something you need to use as an affirmation.

The Prayers are not so much about creating energy, as about accessing the energy of your Mind or Heart, as it is now, and bringing about a change in consciousness which takes you up to ever - higher levels of consciousness. There can be great resistance to these changes in consciousness, because the Ego, does not want to relinquish control. This resistance can happen at any level, even to those in the higher levels of consciousness, who have already ascended to the 5th Dimension and beyond. They still have to be on alert to this energy coming from the Ego, as there are many levels of consciousness that need to be experienced, learned from, cleared, etc., before one can attain the level of God Consciousness found at the Godhead.

While we are in the physical body, we have the Ego, even though we also have the True-Self, our Divine I AM Presence within us, the Ego (personality) is still present and is learning from the True-Self, our I AM Presence, how to be the truth of who we are. We still have to keep the Ego from being in control and allow the True-Self, our Divine I AM Presence within us, to guide our actions and reactions to be Unconditional Love.

We are all being challenged to grow to ever higher levels of Consciousness. The way is different for each one. In the development of these Prayers, many different types of messages had to be conveyed, to many different types of Mind Consciousness.

As the developer of these Prayers, which have been designed to aid the consciousness of Humanity to evolve to Cosmic Ascension, the task has been a delight and also an amazing experience. As such, I feel honored to have been of service in this manner during this incarnation.

The Prayers are meant to Challenge you. As you go higher in consciousness, you will find that you have become the Prayers, and the information contained within the Prayers is within you, within your Consciousness, within your Spirit/Soul, within your Physical Body, Body Elemental and Inner Child.

With this understanding, you will no longer feel compelled to read the prayers as often, or feel any energy from the prayers, as the emotional charges that were negative, have either been changed to positive energy or have disappeared. As you dealt with the energy's density, and cleared enough of the negative energy, you are able to relax and be still. Or if the negative energy is still there, the energy charge in any given situation is greatly decreased.

The energy is not created by the Prayers; so much as the Prayers access the energy that is within you. With your connection to the Key Prayers for Cosmic Ascension, you have become one with them, and you are that. You are the Prayers, and the Prayers in consciousness have become part of you.

In achieving the Higher Consciousness that is at the higher end of the 4th Dimension and into the 5th Dimension, the Prayers help you shift to the Consciousness necessary for entry into the 5th Dimension. They aid you in the clearance, clarity, enlightenment, and acceptance of the Divine Perfection that you are.

In the attainment of the 5ᵗʰ Dimensional energies and Beyond, the Prayers can help you deal with the challenges and changes that are happening for you.

Continued use of the Prayers, or select Paragraphs or Phrases from the Prayers will assist you as situations arise and in the maintenance of the Higher Consciousness that you have achieved. These Prayers etc. will be ones that appeal to your Mind and Heart. You have within you the format, techniques and skills necessary to formulate prayers that suit the level of consciousness that you are at now in your evolution.

How to Use This Book

There are many ways in which you may wish to use this book:

Read the Prayer slowly and feel the Prayer from your Heart Energy.

Read the Prayer, speaking it aloud, begin slowly and repeat the prayer while gradually speeding up the tempo a bit; so that the energy, vibration and frequency are uplifted.

When Reading Prayers as a group participant – be certain that you read them aloud and at the same pitch of voice and tempo as others in the group;

Be Mindful and Heartfelt at what thoughts and feelings come up for you when you are saying the Prayers; or after having said the Prayers, notice what thoughts and feelings come through to your conscious awareness during the day.

Observe what thoughts and feelings come through for you during the weeks that follow, especially if you are saying the same Prayers consistently, as in each morning or evening.

Read, Speak and Write an affirmation three times and then repeat it three more times during the day for 28 days; this is a powerful exercise.

Notice what issues and problems you desire to have healed, and choose the Prayers, that have the attributes for the healing.

Whenever you have an issue or problem occurring during your day, bring in the Sacred Flame of Healing that would cover that issue or problem, and ask your Mighty I AM Presence to remove the negative energy from that issue or problem, and to ensure that you attain the level of Wisdom and Understanding needed that can clear this issue or problem from your Mind and Emotions.

You must consciously change a Negative Belief to a Positive Belief in order to achieve the Positive Cause that leads to the Positive Effects. Your Mighty I AM Presence can help you choose the new Positive belief that brings about the desired change.

The Sacred Flames and Rays can help you achieve the necessary Wisdom and Understanding that will clear the limiting beliefs from you; be sure to ask your Mighty I AM Presence to remove the negative energy from your four body systems. The four body systems consists of; The Physical Body, Etheric Body, Mental and Emotional Body and the Spirit/Soul.

Ask your Mighty I AM Presence to receive the negative energy from you, so that it can then be transmuted, transformed and transfigured to positive energy that will benefit you, the Planet Earth and Humanity.

When you read the Prayers to yourself, listen into your thought processes and your feelings, and notice what comes up for you. Your mind may wander - this being avoidance of some part of the Prayer. It may be a word or a sentence that contains something that the mind does not want to think about - because of the triggers contained within the unconscious mind that lead to belief systems that are out of consciousness, and therefore of the unconscious.

Be aware of any physical charge of energy - no matter how large or small that charge of energy may be - and what thoughts or emotions preceded that charge. The charge of energy is a trigger to what is occurring within your unconscious mind, an indicator that there is something here for you to investigate.

Notice any mental or emotional distractions that occur for you when reading the Prayers, such as, loss of focus or lack of comprehension. These distractions represent issues that need to be addressed. In so doing you will develop a greater understanding of what is happening within your unconscious mind.

Realize that we manifest in our lives the dis-ease of our mental and emotional state, which thus creates our physical disease or wellness. The dis-ease of the Mind, (mental and emotions), creates the diseases within our physical body.

(Repeat the Prayer in a series of three.) Followed by the prayer - Prayer to the Subconscious Mind, (page 46)

Each time you repeat a prayer, you build a momentum of Light encoded in the prayer.

This enables the Prayer to change the Subconscious Mind

Speak your Prayers from your Heart, because your Heart is connected to your Higher-Mind, your Higher-Self, which in turn connects you to your I AM Presence, the Lord God essence of your being.

The Mind is connected to the Left Brain, the consciousness of the lower mind.

The Heart is connected to the Right Brain, the consciousness of the higher mind, enabling access to the All-Knowing of Higher Consciousness and your I AM Presence.

Observe your thoughts and feelings, your belief systems, patterns and programs. Apply the Sacred Flames and Rays that can help you achieve the necessary Wisdom and Understanding that will help clear these limiting beliefs from you. Be sure to ask your mighty I AM Presence to remove the negative energy from your four body system.

Ask your mighty I AM Presence to receive the negative energy from you so, that it can then be transmuted, transformed and transfigured to positive energy that will then benefit the Planet and Humanity.

Questions to ask one's self when you have an emotional reaction.

What is the emotion that I am feeling?

What is the cause of this emotion? What thoughts and feelings preceded this emotional reaction?

What is the reason for the emotion?

What is behind the emotion? And is there anything else, anything more?

When thinking back over my life, when was the first time I felt this emotion, this feeling of...?

What was happening to or for me at the time?

What was being said to me then?

What did I make this event or what happened, mean about me?

What prevents me from being or achieving ...?

Next ask yourself these questions

Am I ready to heal this emotion?

Is there any part of me that does not want to heal this emotion?

If so, what is the positive reason for this part of me holding onto this emotion?

Have a conversation with this part of you, and explain to it, that you are okay, that it is time to heal and let go, to release the old negative programs and their energy, and rewrite their meanings to new positive and heartfelt ones; manifesting new programs that will enhance your life and expand your consciousness, creating a joyful and successful experience.

Ask these additional questions:

Have I achieved the Understanding and Wisdom needed about these emotions and reactions?

What Understanding and Wisdom do I still need in order to be able to move on?

What belief about myself is blocking me from achieving my desires?

What prevents me from being …?

Write an affirmation that changes the meaning from a negative causal belief to a positive causal belief.

Examples: <u>I am unworthy, to I AM Worthy</u>. <u>I am a bad person, to I AM a Good person</u>, If possible, keep your affirmation simple and easy to remember, so that you can instantly reframe the negative thoughts and emotions to positive thoughts and emotions, as they come into your awareness of your mind's consciousness.

Ask your Mighty I AM Presence to receive all the negative energies contained within your Spirit/Soul Being, on all levels of your four Body Systems that relate to the negative thoughts and emotions. Then have the Sacred Violet Flame transmuted and transform this negative energy into Freedom, Forgiveness and Unconditional Love.

Always ask your Mighty I AM Presence, for the Wisdom and Understanding in any situation, And that all of this information is for your highest good, and the highest good of all.

Beloved One, as you read these prayers, feel their messages, and observe how you are touched within your Heart-Mind by their power and magical healing:

I ask that you envisage yourself contained within a circle of fire, formed by the Sacred Flame. To feel the Flame surround you, encapsulating your entire being within its vibrant energy, and as these energies entwine and merge around you, permeating every particle of your being, feel and know from your Heart-Mind that the attributes and qualities of these Flames are healing you and are creating changes into your life, along with the greater Understanding and Wisdom that you require.

Surrender to the possibilities and they become actualities. Allow the Flames to permeate and saturate you entirely. Simply be in their energy and trust.

The Sacred Flames and Rays are energized from the Source that is The One, the Ultimate, and Supreme God of All Creations, the All That Is. They are one of the greatest gifts that have been bestowed upon Humanity in our lifetime. They are for the healing of all Humanity, all Kingdoms and Realms of Planet Earth, this Universe the Multiverses and the Omniverse.

Know that when you call upon the Sacred Flames and Rays of Christed Light of God Consciousness, they come to your aid instantly and begin their wondrous healing and guidance immediately.

Surrender your doubts to your Mighty I AM Presence and Invoke the Sacred Flames and Rays of the Will of God and Illumination. This will enable you to surrender, let go and receive the Wisdom and Understanding needed for you Inner Growth.

Ask for and allow the Sacred Flames and Rays to be with you, in you and surround your life with Healing, Guidance, Wisdom and Understanding, and then All in your life will be Divine Perfection.

If you discover any resistance to the idea of the Sacred Flames and Rays being within you and around your auric field, call in your Mighty I AM Presence, and request that you receive the Wisdom and Understanding about this resistance. What it is all about? What part of you is rejecting the aid of the Sacred Flames and Rays? What is the purpose of this resistance?

Work with this part of you and explain the Positive Benefits of the Sacred Flames and Rays. In that they can bring healing for your Mental, Emotional and Physical Well-being, as well as Spiritual Growth. They can help to resurrect you to the New Encodement of Divine Perfection, as decreed by The One, the Ultimate and Supreme God of All Creations.

The Sacred Flames and Rays have the Power to help you, but you are the one that has to make the decision on what help you desire.

The Sacred Flames and Rays do not make the choices for you. It is all done in accordance with your Divine Will for this incarnation. The Divine Will of your Spiritual God-Self that is your True-Self, has the plan for your lifestream and evolution, and ensures that everything needed for your life is manifested as required.

The Power of Surrender:

What does surrender mean?

Surrender means: Relinquishing, Handing over, Releasing, Letting Go and the Giving to, a Power Source - such as one's Mighty I AM Presence, to Mother/Father God, or to the Sacred Flames and Rays, - an Issue, Problem, Belief System, Pattern, Program, Negative Energy etc., that you desire to cleanse, clear, balance and harmonize, and to receive the Clarity, Wisdom and Understanding you require as you go forward in your evolution.

The Self-Empowerment comes from the Feeling of Freedom, Forgiveness and Unconditional Love that Surrender brings to your Spirit/Soul, Heart, Mind/Emotions and Physical Body. As such you release, handover or relinquish all that which no longer serves you.

In the Power of Surrender, be in Gratitude for all the Learnings you have received and Experiences you have endured, because of your belief systems, patterns, programs and past-life Akashic records that have been held within your cellular memory, having given you great Wisdom and Understanding, these are an important part of who you are and why you are here on Planet Earth at this point in time. Also they will give you the directions for where you are to go next in your journey.

Prayer to Release and Relinquish to the Divine Light of Source

I Surrender and Relinquish to the Divine Light of Source, the All That Is, all the negative energies contained within my being, my Spirit energy, my four Body Systems of Spirit/Soul, Mind/Emotion, Etheric and Physical Body - that have kept me in fear.

I Surrender and Relinquish to the Divine Light of Source, the All That Is, the Akashic Records of all my Past Lives that I have ever lived, including this current life incarnation. All the negative energies that stem from events and incidence of the past are restored to Peace, Balance, Harmony, Unconditional Love, Freedom and Forgiveness.

I Surrender and Relinquish to the Divine Light of Source, the All That Is, all the Drama and Stories that are held within my Subconscious Mind, I AM Living Free and I AM Forgiven for all the beliefs of transgressions against myself and toward others that I have held energetically within my beingness.

I Invoke the Sacred Flames and Rays to transmute and transform all meanings, beliefs, patterns and programs contained within my Mind/Emotions, to the Balance and Harmony of the Divine Perfection that is the Holy Spirit of God.

"Love Is All That Is! And ... So It Is!"

Key Prayers for Cosmic Ascension

The Sacred Flames and Rays of

God Consciousness

Sacred Flame and Ray of the Will of God – Image yourself within a Circle of Radiant Blue Flames at the core center of the Sacred Flame and Ray of the Will of God Surrender to the Divine Principles of The One, the Supreme Creator God.

Ray 1 – The Blue Ray

The Sacred Flame of the Will of God

Elohim: Hercules and Amazonia

Chohan: Master El Morya

Archangel: Michael

Divine Complement: Lady Faith

Key Attributes:

Courage, Faith, Initiative, Dependability, Divine Power, Omnipotence, the Will of God, Self-reliance, Surrender, Focus, Protection and Certainty;

Sacred Flame Energy Amplified on Monday

Divine Principles of The One, the Ultimate and Supreme God of All Creations

The Will of God!

Prayer to the Chohan: Master El Morya for Guidance

Beloved Master El Morya, Chohan of the Blue Ray and the Sacred Flame of the Will of God, Great Spiritual Hierarch of the Brotherhood of the Diamond Heart, and Hierarch of the Temple of Good Will.

I Call upon you to assist me in my desire to Surrender to the Will of God, and to hold within my being the Divine attributes of the Blue Ray – which are courage, faith, initiative, dependability, divine power, self-reliance and certainty. These are the qualities of the Divine Principle of The One, the Ultimate, Supreme God of All Creation, the All That Is.

I Invoke the Holy Spirit of the Christed Light of God Consciousness; that I AM the embodiment of these attributes. I AM spiritually focused and disciplined in applying to my life the Divine teachings of the Blue Ray, and I Request the aid of the Blue Flame Angels to protect and guard me in my journey of exploration within myself.

I AM One with the Heart of God and I AM aware that I AM held within the embrace of the Unconditional Love of All That Is.

Beloved Master El Morya, I Thank You for your service and life in guarding and protecting the spiritual heart centers of the world, in all areas of movement and spiritual growth that will bring into manifestation the changes that will restore the human race to peace and harmony, and advance the evolution of Humanity.

Thy Will IS Done, Thy Will IS Done, and Thy Will IS Done, in this Now Moment. Thank you, Beloved Master El Morya. "And… So It Is!"

Prayer of Surrender to the Will of God for Humanity

Beloved Mighty I AM Presence, Lord God essence of my being, I Call upon Master El Morya, Chohan of the Sacred Flame and Ray of the Will of God, Hierarch of the Temple of Good Will; Hercules and Amazonia, Elohim of the First Ray; the Lords of Karma, the Great Divine Director: Master Ragoczy and the Beloved Lady Quan Yin, Lady Nada, Lady Pallas Athena, Lady Portia, Goddess of Liberty; and the Beloved Cyclopea, Elohim of the Fifth Ray.

I Ask the Archangel Michael and the Divine Complement Lady Faith of the First Ray to be present and for ALL to come forth and be in charge and guardianship of the Surrender to the Will of God of ALL of Humanity in this now moment of time.

I Ask that Humanity come to see the truth of who they are, and awaken to the Divine Truth of The One, the Ultimate, Supreme God of All Creation, and thereby surrender to the Divine Will of God, and to the Divine Plan of God the Creator for ALL of Humanity, ALL the Kingdoms and Realms of Earth and for Planet Earth in her Ascension to her rightful place in this Universe, and to the Ascension of Humanity into the 5th Dimension and Beyond.

I Invoke the Universal Laws of One Unity Consciousness, which will cause Humanity to remember the Holy Spirit of The One, the Ultimate, Supreme God of All Creation; the All That Is. To bring Humanity home to the All-Knowing of the eternal Unconditional Love and Abundance, which is their birthright, and to be in Trust of the Truth and Transparency of The One, the Ultimate, Supreme God of All Creation.

In God I Trust, Now and forever.
Beloved I AM! "And... So It Is!"

Prayer for Personal Surrender

I AM in total surrender to my Mighty I AM Presence. I AM in total surrender to The One, the Ultimate and Supreme God of All Creations, the All That Is.

I AM focused and committed to surrender all my wilfulness and negative mental and emotional pain. I AM One with God, in total surrender to the Heart, Mind and Will of God.

I AM disciplined in all the things that I AM.

I AM responsible in all the things that I AM.

I AM committed to all the things that I AM.

I AM on All Levels of my Being, encapsulated by the Divine Holy Spirit of All That Is; The Holy Spirit permeates every molecule, cell, atom, proton and electron of my Soul and my four Body Systems, with the Christed Light of God Consciousness of All That Is.

I AM Freedom in my Surrender, as I Trust in the Truth of my Mighty I AM Presence. I AM Free and Surrender to the New Blueprint and Encodement of the Divine Perfection that I AM.

Beloved I AM! "And... So It Is!"

Prayer of Surrender to My I Am Presence

I Surrender all my fear – related thoughts, feelings and emotions that are held within me on all levels of my being – my Soul, Spirit, Mind and Body, Etheric Body, All Subtle Bodies, Body Elemental and Inner Child – to my Beloved Mighty I AM Presence, the Lord God essence of my being.

All Belief Systems, Patterns and Programs relating to Fear and the creation of negative energies are removed from me now.

I Surrender these Belief Systems, Patterns and Programs to my Mighty I AM Presence, to be transmuted and transformed to the Divine Perfection and Unconditional Love Energy of The One, the Ultimate and Supreme God of all Creations, in the knowledge that these energies are used for my Highest Good and the Highest Good of All.

I AM Healed of all negative fear – based programs, they are resolved, and there is Divine Love, Harmony, Balance and Peace within my Heart, Soul, Spirit, my four Body Systems, All Subtle Bodies, Body Elemental and Inner Child.

Beloved I AM! "And... So It Is!"

Prayer for Protection

I AM protected always by the Will of God.
I AM protected by my Mighty I AM Presence.
I Call upon the Sacred Flame and Ray of the Will of God to
Saturate my beingness with waves upon waves of Blue Flame Fire.
I AM positive in all situations and I speak my truth. I AM
calm and in discernment no matter what is said to me.
I AM in my Power and Empowered by my Divinity.
I Stay true to my inner self and my inner guidance.
I Remain peaceful, tranquil and compassionate in the now moment.
I Embrace the Energy of the Blue Flame Angels of Protection.
The Blue Flame Angels protect and guard my beingness, as I go
forth in life; I AM courageous, faithful, in control of my Destiny.
I AM strong and I AM my Spiritual God-Self State. I AM the
Love of my Holy Christed Light Self. Beloved Archangel Michael
and the Divine Complement Lady Faith: I Thank You for your
Guidance and Wisdom. I AM in Gratitude for Your Protection and
the Protection of the Sacred Blue Flames and Rays of God's Will.
I AM protected in all areas of my life. Protected I AM! "And... So Is It!"

Invocation to the Elohim: Hercules and Amazonia of the Will of God Flame and Ray

I Invoke the Elohim: Hercules and Amazonia, of the Sacred Flame and Ray of the Will of God, to make manifest into this world on Planet Earth a gigantic wave of the Will of God Flame. To encircle this planet and encapsulate and permeate every particle of All Life Forms and All Life Forces of this Sacred Planet Earth – to Surrender to the Will of God and to the Divine Principles of God's Will.

The Divine Plan for Planet Earth in accordance with the Divine Will of The One, the Ultimate and Supreme God of All Creations, the All That Is, shall be manifested in this now moment of time.

The New Encodements which have been development for Planet Earth, and the Universe, are installed, revivified and resurrected in accordance to the Divine Principles of God's Will.

I AM the Resurrection and the Life; I AM the Resurrection and the Life, I AM the Resurrection and the Life of the New Encodements of Divine Perfection for Planet Earth, and the Universe, in Accordance to the Divine Principles of God's Will for Planet Earth and the Universe..

I AM in Gratitude for the Protection that has emanated from the Elohim Hercules and Amazonia, for Planet Earth, the Universe and All the Kingdoms and Realms of Planet Earth.

I Give Thanks to the Elohim for the Light that has sustained and maintained the Light Life Force for Mother Earth, in keeping with the Divine Will and Principles of the Creator of All That Is. I AM in Acceptance of All That Is as Divine Perfection in Action, according to the Divine Will of God. Thank you, Elohim of the Sacred Flame and Ray of God's Will.

"And.... So It Is!"

Prayer: The Sword of Archangel Michael

Beloved Archangel Michael, the Protector and Guardian for Planet Earth and Humanity, I Reach out to you in these times of great change and challenges, to connect with you and the great energy that you hold, as the Bearer of the Sword of Light and Truth that protects us all. Bringing greater Understanding and Wisdom in the ways of Acceptance and the Divine Perfection that is God's Will.

I Feel from the Sacred Chambers of my Heart a Desire so Profound, and a Power-Divine, to be the embodiment of the Sword of Michael, the Sword of Light and Truth, so that I may walk with you, a Protector of the Innocent Children that are Humanity, being the Light of Truth and myself, a Beacon of Light, setting the World afire, within the Blue Flame Light Of God's Will and Words of Truth.

I AM in Service to Mother/Father God. I AM in Service to you. I offer myself to be an instrument of your service, in the Protection and Guardianship of Humanity and All the Kingdoms and Realms of Planet Earth.

We are One – We are the Suns of The One.
Beloved We Are. "And... So It Is!"

Prayer to Archangel Michael and the Divine Complement Lady Faith

Beloved Archangel Michael and the Divine Complement Lady Faith, I AM in Gratitude for your dedication to the Evolution of Humanity. I Honor you for your involvement in the Protection of Humanity and All the Kingdoms and Realms of Planet Earth throughout eons of time.

I Call upon you, in this period of Planet Earth's Cosmic Ascension to the 5th Dimension and Beyond, to be my Mentor, Guide and Guardian in how I AM in Christed Light of God Consciousness, best able to be of Divine Service to The One, the Ultimate, Supreme God of All Creation, the All That Is, as a Protector and Keeper of the Sacred Flames and Rays of God's Will upon the surface of Planet Earth.

I AM in Gratitude and Thank you for all that you have done and Continue to do for our Beloved Planet Earth.

Blessings of Divine Love and Cosmic Light are with you always.

"And... So It Is!"

Prayer to the Angels of God's Will

Beloved Archangel Michael, the Divine Complement Lady Faith and all the Angels of God's Will; I AM One with You. We are in Oneness and Unity.

I Surrender to the Will of God. I AM embraced by your vibrations and frequencies of Protection, Trust, Courage and All the Qualities contained within the Divine Principles of God's Holy Will for my life.

I Feel your Presence and Protection in all areas of my Life. I Trust your Guidance as you help me to be in Complete Surrender to God's Will.

All Paradigms and Beliefs Systems held within me have been changed to Positive Causal Beliefs and the Qualities of the Divine Principles of God's Will.

I AM therefore Courageous, Self-Reliant, my Spiritual God-Self and have Faith and Trust in God's Holy Will for my Life.

I AM in Gratitude Archangel Michael, Lady Faith and All the Angels of God's Will, for your Love and Faith in me and I Thank You for All your Guidance and help. Your Love, Wisdom and Understanding have shown me the correct pathway to Cosmic Ascension. I Now see that God's Will is my Will. I AM in Oneness with God. I AM in Oneness with my Spiritual God-Self; the Will of God is within me.

"And... So It Is!"

Sacred Flame and Ray of Illumination – Image yourself within a Circle of Illuminating Yellow Flame at the core center of the Sacred Flame and Ray of Illumination Experience the Expansion of Wisdom and Understanding that is the Mind of God.

Ray 2 – The Yellow Ray

The Sacred Flame of Illumination

Elohim: Apollo and Lumina

Chohans: Lord Lanto and Master Kuthumi

Archangel: Jophiel

Divine Complement: Christine

Key Attributes:

Illumination, Wisdom, Understanding through Love, Truth, Integrity, Omniscience, Transparency, Perceptions, Precipitations, Discrimination, Discernment and the Activation of the Mind of God;

Sacred Flame Energy Amplified on Sunday

The Expansion of Wisdom and Understanding through

the Unconditional Love of Self and Others

The Mind of God!

Prayer to the Chohan:
Lord Lanto and Master Kuthumi

Beloved Lord Lanto, Master Kuthumi and the Beloved Masters and Lady Masters of the Sacred Flame and Ray of Illumination; as I Reflect and be in the quiet times of my life, I Wonder at the magnitude of the Will of God. I Ask myself the questions: Who am I? What am I here in this Life to learn? And how do I go about this learning? I Recall and Remember in my mind and heart that you, the Chohan and Master Teachers, have held the Sacred Flame and Ray of Illumination alive for Humanity and Planet Earth for eons of time. I AM in deepest Gratitude for your Fortitude and Great Love for us All.

I Request your Guidance, as I seek the answers to my questions and go forth on my quest for greater understanding of myself – to experience, to see, to feel and to hear, and thereby gain the Wisdom and Understanding that I require from my learning. From which I then move forward and Let Go and Let God receive from me all energies that no longer serve me. I AM the Wisdom and understanding and I AM able to attain, sustain and maintain the Illumination Energy within my being, from the Sacred Flame and Ray of Illumination.

I Call upon you to advise me in all matters of Communication, within myself to my Inner Child and Body Elemental, with my Beloved Mighty I AM Presence, with All Humankind and All the Kingdoms and Realms of Planet Earth.

I AM pledged to be of Service to The One, the Ultimate and Supreme God of All Creations. I Request that I be counselled by you in all matters pertaining to my communication with the Holy Spirit. I AM in Gratitude for my Wisdom and Understanding. I Give Thanks for the wise counsel that I AM receiving in this now moment of time. I AM in Gratitude for ALL the Guidance and Light bestowed upon me, from you, Beloved Lord Lanto, Master Kuthumi, All the Masters and Lady Masters and the Archangels of the Sacred Flame and Ray of Illumination. Beloved I AM! "And... So It Is!"

Prayer to the Sacred Flame and Ray of Illumination

Beloved One, the Ultimate and Supreme God of All Creations, the All That Is, the Beloved Chohan: Master Kuthumi. Beloved Lord Lanto and the beloved Masters of the Sacred Flame and Ray of Illumination and Wisdom;

As the Sacred Flame and Ray embraces my Heart, Mind and Emotions, my Spirit, Soul, four Body Systems and all Subtle Bodies, Body Elemental and Inner Child, I Feel the Illumination and Transformation of all that is not of the Divine Light from my being, to the Wisdom, Understanding and the Unconditional Love that is the Illumination of Truth.

All Illusion within me is Released from my being, so that I AM my Divinity in Christed Light of God Consciousness. My Beloved Mighty I AM Presence is my Reality and my life is transformed to be the Heart, Mind and Will of the Beloved One, the Ultimate and Supreme God of All Creations, the All That Is.

My Spirit, Soul, four Body Systems, all Subtle Bodies, Body Elemental and Inner Child, have the Light Quotient levels within raised in degrees that ensure my healing with ease and grace. The Light Quotient levels once raised are permanently locked in.

Beloved I AM! "And... So It Is!"

Prayer for the Illumination of Planet Earth

Beloved Cosmic Logos: Avatar of Synthesis: the Mahatma. Beloved Universal Logos: Lord Melchizedek. The Universal Hierarchy; Beloved Planetary Logos: Lord Gautama Buddha. Planetary Hierarchy: Lord Sanat Kumara and Lady Venus. Beloved Planetary Christ: Lord Maitreya. The Great Divine Director: Master Ragoczy. The Universal Judge; the Maha Chohan: Master St. Germain. Chohan: Master Kuthumi and Lord Lanto of the Sacred Flame and Ray of illumination – and the Archangel Jophiel and Lady Christine.

I Call upon you to encapsulate Planet Earth within a circle of Illumination Fire, the Sacred Flame and Ray of Illumination, so that every particle, atom, molecule, cell, proton, electron and DNA that forms Planet Earth and its inhabitants are immersed within the Illumination Fire of Wisdom, Understanding and Truth.

All Humankind and All the Kingdoms and Realms that live on or within Planet Earth, down to the very Core of Planet Earth, are immersed in the Light of Illumination. The Truth is revealed to All about this Great and Beautiful Planet – Our Home, that it is a Living entity and a wonderful, benevolent Goddess and Mother to us ALL.

The Earth, the Air, the Fire and the Water Elements of Planet Earth, are cleansed and cleared of all negative toxins and beliefs systems that are not of the Illumination Ray of Truth. The Sacred Flame and Ray of Ascension and Purification, along with the Sacred Flame and Ray of Healing and Manifestation, aid Planet Earth in this Healing process – as they bring in the Divine Energy of God Consciousness, through the Sacred Flames and Rays, to Rejuvenate and Connect Planet Earth to the New Encodements of Divine Perfection. The Holy Spirit of Christed Light of God Consciousness encapsulates and permeates all of Planet Earth, and All the Kingdom and Realms of Planet Earth, within the Cosmic Christed Light Energies of The One, the All That Is. "And... So It Is!"

Invocation of the Sacred Flame
and Ray of Illumination

I AM my Beloved Mighty I AM. I Hereby Invoke the Sacred Flame and Ray of Illumination to enhance my focus upon the Mind of God daily, and in all matters – in my thought processes, perceptions, comprehension, precipitation and discernment. Expand my Wisdom to the higher perspectives and consciousness of the Holy Spirit, the Mind of God.

The Mind of God within me is Activated, and All my Decisions and the manner in which I Conduct my Life, are always in ways that bring me Wisdom, Understanding and Unconditional Love, with ease and grace.

Elohim: Apollo and Lumina. Lord Lanto, Master Kuthumi and Lord Gautama Buddha of the Sacred Flame and Ray of Illumination, Invoke and Amplify the Mind of God within my Mind.

I AM the Mind of God. In the Sacred Chambers of my Heart, I know and feel that this is for my Highest Good and the Highest Good of All.

I AM in Gratitude for the Amplification of the Sacred Flame and Ray of Illumination; I AM One with the Holy Spirit, the Mind of God.

I AM Illumination blazing Now!

"And... So It Is!"

Prayer to the Subconscious Mind

My Beloved Subconscious Mind, I send Blessings of Love to thee.

I Hereby Ask and Command that you take all the thought forms of my prayers, with all the higher consciousness levels of energy and Vital Light and Vital Godforce contained within that are needed and necessary, to manifest and demonstrate these prayers, to the Source of my being through my Beloved Monad and Mighty I AM Presence.

(Wait 30 seconds)

Visualize or have a felt sense of the prayers Vital Light and Godforce energy, streaming up through your Crown Chakra and Source Star like a geyser of the Multi-colored United Rays of God Consciousness, to the Source of all life, the All That Is.

(Next say aloud)

Lord, let the Golden Rain of Blessings Fall.
God's Will is done on Earth as it is in Heaven!
"And... So It Is!"

Prayer for Wisdom and
Understanding in All Situations

In all that I say and do, in all situations, my Actions are forever true in Light, Love, Wisdom and Understanding.

I express myself with the words and sounds of Compassion, Wisdom and Understanding.

Archangel of Illumination and Wisdom, Jophiel and the Divine Complement Lady Christine, accompany me in my daily life, and Guide me always toward the Light of the Heart of All-Knowing, the Heart of Reasoning and Compassion.

I AM guided by you, I AM Focused and attentive to the Truth of the Illumination that you bring unto me, and I follow your examples.

I leave a footprint of Light and Love in every area of my life.

In all that I say and do, in all situations, my Actions are forever Truthful, Honest and in Integrity – the actions of the Angelic Realms of Illumination are within me.

I AM in Gratitude to Beloved Archangel Jophiel and Lady Christine for the Illumination of Wisdom and Divine Understanding that you exemplify.

Beloved I AM! "And... So It Is!"

Invocation to the Elohim: Apollo and Lumina for Illumination

Beloved Elohim: Apollo and Lumina of the Sacred Flame and Ray of Illumination, Wisdom and Understanding.

I Invoke the energy of the Illumination Flame and Ray into my life to transform by the Light of the Mind of God, the New Encodements, (the building blocks) contained within all levels of my being – to the Divine Mind of God.

All beliefs, patterns and programs held within my Mind, Mental and Emotional that serve me not are Transfigured to the Divine Illumination of the Light of Wisdom, Understanding and Love.

All negative energies that have permeated my physical body – and are therefore stored within my energy fields – are released unto the Light Realms and are Transformed to positive energy, with the Intention that this Energy may be used for the Highest Good of Planet Earth, Humanity and All the Kingdoms and Realms of Earth.

Beloved Elohim: Apollo and Lumina. I AM Eternally Grateful for your Light of Illumination, which surrounds Planet Earth with waves upon waves of the Sacred Flaming Fires of Illumination; and also for the Cosmic Rays of Illumination to assist Mother Earth and also to keep alive the Sacred Flame and Ray for the Highest Good of Planet Earth, Humanity and All the Kingdoms and Realms of Earth.

Thank you, Beloved Ones; for all that you have done for Planet Earth, Humanity and All the Kingdoms and Realms of Planet Earth.

Beloved I AM. "And... So It Is!"

Prayer to Archangel Jophiel and the Divine Complement Lady Christine

My Beloved Mighty I AM Presence, Lord God essence of my being, be within me now. I Request the presence of the Archangel Jophiel and the Divine Complement Lady Christine, to be with me in this now moment of time, to help me understand with Love the many problems that beset me, and lower my thoughts and feelings into energy that is the opposite of Love.

I Ask of you in this time of Depressed Emotions, for the Comprehension and Perceptions that will best assist me in attaining; Clarity, Wisdom and Understanding.

I AM Open to receive from you the Wisdom and Knowledge that will be for my Highest Good and the Highest Good of all in these situations. Then I AM Free and Ready to be of Service to The Holy Spirit, the Mind of God. The All That Is!

I AM That I AM!
"And… So It Is!"

Prayer to the Angels of Illumination

Beloved Archangel Jophiel, the Divine Complement Lady Christine and All the Angels of the Sacred Flame and Ray of Illumination; I Feel your Vibrant Frequency Energies of Wisdom, Understanding and Love, as they surround and permeate every level of my being.

Because of your Love, I AM Whole and Complete. I AM Connected in Oneness to the Truth and Integrity of the Mind of God within my God-Self. I AM my Mighty I AM Presence.

I Thank You for Illuminating my Thoughts and Emotions, so I AM Aware of my Thinking and Feelings in this now moment of time already, because of the Wisdom, Understanding and Love you have shown me.

I AM able to Create Positive Causal Effects, which have changed my Life to Balance and Harmony of my Mind, the Mind of God within. I AM bringing Balance and Harmony to myself, others and to the Consciousness of Humanity.

I AM in Gratitude for your Transparency, Knowledge, Illumination, Wisdom, Understanding and Love of the Mind of God.

I AM Perceptive, and show Discernment and Compassion in All Areas of my Life, for this I AM Eternally Grateful.

Thank You Archangel Jophiel, Lady Christine and All the Angels of Illumination; I See through the Illusion, I Know the Truth of Who I AM. I AM an Enlightened Spiritual Soul and I Know this has ever been so.

I AM Divine Perfection. I AM the Illumination of the Mind of God already, because I AM That I AM! I AM All That Is.

"And... So It Is!"

Sacred Flame of Cosmic Love – Sacred Crystal-Rose Flame of Cosmic Love: Image yourself within a Circle of Pulsating Pink Flame at the core center of the Sacred Flame and Ray of Cosmic Love, Connect with the Sacred Chambers of your Heart and Be Love.

Ray 3: The Pink Ray

The Sacred Flame of Cosmic Love

The Crystal Rose Quartz

Elohim: Heros and Amora

Chohan: Master Paul the Venetian

Archangel: Chamuel

Divine Complement: Lady Charity

Key Attributes:

Divine Self-Love, Unconditional Cosmic Love: the Key to Multiplication, Love of Others, Compassion, Mercy, Charity, True Brotherhood of the Spirit, Wisdom of the Heart of All Knowing, Open Heartedness, and Living from the Heart: the Sacred Chambers of the Heart.

Sacred Flame Energy Amplified on Tuesday

The Three-fold Flame within the Heart

The Heart of God!

Prayer to the Chohan: Master Paul the Venetian

Beloved Master Paul the Venetian, Chohan for the Sacred Flame and Ray of Cosmic Love. With the Grace of the Holy Spirit, I welcome you into my Heart and Feelings, to reside within me on all levels of my being, across all dimensions, time and space.

I Desire of you, the Master of Divine Love, to teach me the pathways to Divine Self-Love that I AM as you are, a Divine expression of Love in ALL that I AM in my Life.

I Request your Guidance and Wisdom in that I AM able to stay within my Truth and Live from my Divine Heart, at all times and during all situations. I AM in need of the Knowledge, Wisdom and Understanding of what prevents me from Living in and from my Divine Heart of Self Love.

I Request of you Beloved One that all the negative energy, pain and trauma that are in my Heart, be revealed unto me, so that I AM able to Release these Energies, to the Sacred Flame and Ray of Cosmic Love. With the Learning and Wisdom attained, I AM the Divine Love that is the Divine Heart of Lemuria.

I Affirm that Master Paul the Venetian, and the Sacred Flame and Ray of Cosmic Love, surround me with waves upon waves of the Crystal Rose Fire. I AM the Divine Love of Self in this now moment of time.

In the name of my Beloved I AM Presence, from the very Heart of God, I Breathe in the Love Energy of the Heart of Lemuria, to encapsulate my Heart, and merge with the Sacred Flame and Ray of Cosmic Love, that is the KEY to the Power of Multiplication and all the Good things that my Heart desires.

I AM a Temple of Divine Love. I AM in Gratitude to my Mighty I AM Presence for this Divine Love. I AM Blessed by the Divine Love of All That Is. "And... So It Is!"

Prayer: I Open My Heart

I Open My Heart to Love; I Open My Spiritual Soul;
I Choose to Live My Life with Love, Love Unconditional.
I Open My Heart to Light; I Open My Spiritual Soul;
I Choose to Live my Life in Light, Enlightened with All Knowing.
I Open My Heart to Truth; I Open My Spiritual Soul;
I Choose to Live My Life in Truth, Just and True I AM.
I Open My Heart to Abundance; I Open My Spiritual Soul;
I Choose to Live My Life in Abundance, endowed with Limitless Supply.
I Open My Heart to the Source of Life; I Open My Spiritual Soul;
I Choose to Live My Life with Source, Infinite Awareness and Trust.
I Open My Heart to My Spiritual Divinity; I Open My Spiritual Soul;
I Choose to Live My Life in My Spiritual Divinity;
I AM My Divine I AM Presence.
I Open My Heart to "I AM," I Open My Spiritual Soul,
I Choose to Live My Life as "I AM," I AM that I AM and All That Is.
I Open My Heart to Oneness; I Open my Spiritual Soul;
I Choose to Live My Life in Oneness.
I AM United in the Oneness of The One, the
Ultimate and Supreme God of All Creations.
I AM My Beloved Divine Spirit Always, Beloved I AM. "And... So It Is!"

Prayer: I AM My Heart

I AM My Heart: I AM Love Loved Unconditionally.
I AM My Heart: I AM Light; I AM Enlightened, Wise,
All Knowing and Understanding.
I AM My Heart: I AM Illumine Truth, Just, Honest and True.
I AM My Heart: I AM Abundant, Endowed with
Limitless Supply and Good Fortune;
I AM My Heart: I AM Trusting My I AM Presence.
I AM My Heart: I AM Infinite, Immortal and Harmonious.
I AM My Heart: I AM My Divine Spiritual I AM Presence.
I AM My Heart: I AM that I AM and All That IS, IS "I AM."
I AM My Heart: I AM in Oneness; I AM One and United with
my Divine Spiritual God-Self.
I AM My Heart: I AM Manifesting my Heart's
Desires, Oneness with All That Is.
I AM My Heart Always. "And... So It Is!"

Invocation to the Sacred Flame
and Ray of Cosmic Love

I Call upon the Beloved Elohim: Heros and Amora; Beloved Maha Chohan: Master St. Germain. Beloved Chohan: Master Paul the Venetian of the Sacred Flame and Ray of Cosmic Love, All the Masters and Lady Masters of the Temple of Divine Love, the Archangel; Chamuel and Divine Complement Lady Charity, and All the Angels of Cosmic Love to be with me in this now moment of time.

My Beloved Mighty I AM Presence, Lord God essence of my being, be within me as I Invoke the Sacred Flame and Ray of Cosmic Love to saturate, permeate and infuse every man, woman and child on Planet Earth, with the Cosmic Love from the Heart of God.

I Decree that the glorious Pink Flame and Ray of Cosmic Love encapsulate All Humanity, to restore the Wisdom of the Heart, which encompasses the Wisdom Principles and the Holy Christ Love Principles of the Holy Spirit of the Christed Light of God Consciousness. I acknowledge with the Deepest Love, Respect and Gratitude the Immortal Three-fold Flame of Life cradled within the Sacred Chambers of my Heart. Through the Divine Love that I AM, I direct my Heart Flames to manifest the Divine Plan for my Life.

I AM Pure Divine Love, the True Nature of the Heart of God, the Divine Cosmic Love that is the Power of Creation. I AM the Higher Consciousness of Divine Love. I AM a magnet for Divine Love. I AM radiant with Divine Love. I radiate this Love to All Life Forms and All Force energy.

I AM in Gratitude to my Mighty I AM Presence, my Holy Christ-Self, to my Spirit, Soul and to all aspects of my four Body Systems, my Body Elemental and Inner Child and to all the Elementals of Life.

I Give Thanks to the Elohim: Heros and Amora; to Master Paul the Venetian, to the Archangel Chamuel and the Divine Complement Lady Charity, and to the Legions of Divine Love Angels – for your great Unconditional Love, Compassion, True Brotherhood and Charity.

I AM Divine Love. Therefore, I think feel and respond with Love, I AM Rejuvenated to Divine Cosmic Love and Connected to the New Encodement of Divine Perfection, Beauty, Harmony and Inner Peace.

I AM Cosmic Love! "And... So It Is!"

Prayer of My Heart

I AM the Embodiment of my Monad, and my Mighty I AM Presence.

I AM the Embodiment of my Spirit, and my Beloved Higher Self.

I AM Balanced, Harmonized and in Complete Control of my Life.

I AM the Power of Love and I AM in Love with my Life – from the Sacred Chambers of my Heart, the Center of my Divine Spirituality.

My Heart is Light, my Feet are Light, and my whole Physical Body is Light, Buoyant and Joyous.

I AM my Crystalline Lightbody.

My Heart sings in tune with the Universal Songs of Inner Peace and Harmony.

My Heart sings the songs of Love and Light, lifting up my being to Eternal Life.

My Heart drums to the beat of the Eternal Songs of Gratitude, and the Everlasting songs of Joy and Serenity.

My Heart and Mind are One, and Alive with the energy of All-Knowing and Truth that comes from the Silence, and Oneness with the Cosmic Heart of The One.

My Heart is Open. It pours forth the Pure Unconditional Love and Christed Light of God Consciousness from the Heart of The One; the All That Is.

My Eternal Heart Sings; I AM Love! "And... So It Is!"

Prayer to Anchor the Cosmic Heart, Mind and Will of God into my Heart

Beloved One, the Ultimate and Supreme Mother/Father God of All Creations,

I AM my Mighty I AM Presence. I AM connected to your Cosmic Heart, Mind and Will.

I Anchor my entire beingness within the Sacred Chambers of my Sacred Heart. I AM connected to the Cosmic Heart of The One, the Ultimate and Supreme Mother/father God.

I AM in Oneness with All That Is. I AM Living within my Sacred Heart.

I AM Living from my Sacred Heart Energy, at all times and in all situations.

I Invoke the Antakarana Symbol of the Masculine and Feminine Principles – to be Anchored within my entire Being, my Spirit and Soul, my Mind, my Physical Body and my Heart.

I AM the Embodiment of The One, the Ultimate and Supreme Mother/Father God.

I AM the Embodiment of the Cosmic Heart, Mind and Will of The One, the All That Is.

I AM the Embodiment of my Monad.

I AM the Embodiment of my Mighty I AM Presence.

I AM the Embodiment of my Higher Self.

I AM the Embodiment of my Spirit and Soul, my Mental, Emotional Mind and my Physical Body.

I AM the Embodiment of the Masculine and Feminine Principles, Balanced and in Harmony.

I AM the Embodiment of my Akashic Records.

I AM the Embodiment of Oneness with myself and others.

I AM Anchored Completely within the Sacred Chambers of my Heart,

All that I AM, on ALL levels of my being, is Mirrored unto me in order that the

Activation of Transmutation occurs to Divine Unconditional Love, Forgiveness and Freedom.

I AM the Three-fold Flame within my Heart that brings the

Transformation of All-Knowing, Wisdom and Understanding from the All That Is,

Manifesting for me the Transfiguration of all the negative old beliefs, to positive new beliefs;

Thus this allows for the

Full *Actualization and Amplification of my being*.

In Perfection and the Totality of the Cosmic Heart Energy of The One, the Ultimate and Supreme Mother/Father God of All Creations.

The Masculine and Feminine Energies are in Unconditional Love on all Levels of my being.

I AM Living within my Sacred Heart. I AM Living
from my Sacred Heart Energy, Now and Always. I
Believe in the Blessings of my Sacred Heart.
I Know that all is for my Highest Good and
the Highest Good of the Universe.
"And... So It Is!"

Prayer for the Heart of Humanity

Oh Beloved Master Paul the Venetian, Chohan of the Sacred Flame and Ray of Cosmic Love, I Call unto you to lift up the Hearts of Humanity, in this important time of Humanity's and Planet Earth's history, to restore Humankind to Live from the Heart, the Sacred Chambers of the Heart.

I Desire that Humanity be shown, by the Unconditional Love of the Holy Spirit, the way back to True Brotherhood, Compassion and Charity. And be Love in Action toward all of their brethren – that is Humanity and also toward All the Kingdoms and Realms of Planet Earth.

I Desire the Hearts of Humanity to be open and receptive to the Cosmic Heart of God and to the Divine Love of the Holy Spirit – and therefore made ready to receive the Initiations of the Sacred Heart.

I AM in Gratitude for the Unconditional Love from you, Master Paul the Venetian. This has been demonstrated by your Love in Action and the Love of the Holy Spirit for the Hearts of Humanity and All the Kingdoms and Realms of Planet Earth.

Beloved We Are! "And... So It Is!"

Prayer for Unconditional Love and Compassion

Beloved Chohan: Paul the Venetian. All the Masters and Lady Masters of the Sacred Flame and Ray of Cosmic Love; and all the Angels of the Angelic Realms who serve the Great Crystal Rose Temple of Cosmic Love and my Beloved Mighty I AM Presence.

I Desire from my Heart to Exemplify the Unconditional Love and Compassion that has been demonstrated to all from the Sacred Heart of the Master of Cosmic Love, Master Paul the Venetian.

I AM as the Divine Cosmic Love of Mother/Father God; I AM in the Divine Perfection of Love. I Clear and Cleanse the Veils of Forgetfulness, by emulating the Divine Cosmic Love of the Christed Light of God Consciousness for myself and all aspects of myself.

I AM in Oneness of Cosmic Love for All of Humanity and for All the Kingdoms and Realms with which we share Planet Earth.

I AM in Reverence to the Holy Spirit of Unconditional Love that is the Divine Mother, Lady Gaia/Virgo; Mother Earth.

I AM in Gratitude for all that you have bestowed upon me. I Give thanks for the Blessings of Unconditional Love and Compassion from the Great Temple of Cosmic Love.

Love Is All That Is! "And... So It Is!"

Invocation to the Elohim: Heros and Amore of Cosmic Love

Beloved Elohim: Heros and Amore of the Cosmic Love Flame and Ray, from the depths of my Sacred Heart, I AM Love. I Invoke the Radiant Light of Cosmic Love, to encapsulate All of Humanity and All of the Kingdoms and Realms of Planet Earth.

The Elohim of the Cosmic Love Flame and Ray, the Holy Spirit of Love, that you are, encapsulates Planet Earth with waves upon waves of Cosmic Love Flames. Planet Earth receives the Powerful Cosmic Flame and Ray of Love, lifting her up into the Universe inside Pillars of Cosmic Fire.

Energetically Planet Earth is raised up to be in alignment with all other Planets in the Universe Every man, woman and child of Humanity, and All the Kingdoms and Realms of Planet Earth are permeated, saturated and changed by the Cosmic Flame and Ray of Love, thus they are now able to Connect with the Truth of the Love that they are and have within the Sacred Chambers of their Hearts – for themselves and others and for all beings, whatever their race, creed, color, species, life form or life force energy, that they are able to be Compassionate and Charitable in All situations and to All of Creation.

I Give Thanks to the Elohim: Heros and Amore of the Cosmic Ray and Flame of Love, for all that you do and have done for the Highest Good of Humanity, All the Kingdoms and Realms of Planet Earth and this Universe.

In Cosmic Love I Trust, "And... So It Is!"

Prayer to Archangel Chamuel and the Divine Complement Lady Charity

As I have walked through the days of my life, in this incarnation and lifestream, Archangel Chamuel and the Divine Complement Lady Charity, have shown me the Beauty of my Life. I AM in Appreciation of the Beauty and Artistry of the Mother, Lady Gaia/Virgo and in her creation of all that I experience of this world through my senses of sight, hearing, feeling, touch and the olfactory senses – which are all part of my physical experience of this wonderful world upon which I live and do dwell.

I Love what I see, hear and feel of her that brings to me a sense of Wonderment and Awe at her Power and Majesty.

I AM a Custodian and Guardian for this wonderful world. I pledge to be of Service and light the way so that others will know from their Hearts the Living Life Force that is Mother Earth, Lady Gaia/Virgo.

I hear her Music, the sounds, vibrations and frequencies in which she surrounds us on all levels of our lives.

I hear her Voice and I feel her need of me to be the Truth of Unconditional Love, toward her and All of her Kingdoms and Realms, who are the Children of her Heart.

I AM in Gratitude to the Archangel Chamuel and the Divine Complement Lady Charity, and all the Angels of the Angelic Realms for the Sacred Flame and Ray of Cosmic Love, for their Compassion, Charity and Caring for us all, and in their being the keepers of the Sacred Flame and Ray of Cosmic Love.

I thank you from the Sacred Chambers of my Heart, for keeping this Sacred Flame and Ray of Cosmic Love alive and activated for Mother Earth, "And... So It Is!"

Prayer to the Angels of Cosmic Love

Beloved Archangel Chamuel, the Divine Complement Lady Charity and All the Angels of Cosmic Love;

I AM That I AM and I welcome you into the Sacred Chambers of my Heart and four Body Systems.

The Sacred Chambers of my Heart are Open and the Three-fold Flames within expands to even greater heights and strength. As your presence enters my being – all levels are elevated to Higher Degrees of Conscious Awareness.

Unconditional Self-Love is pulsating throughout my Spirit, Soul, Heart, Mind and All levels of my Physical Body, Extrapolated a Thousand-fold by the Cosmic Love of The One, the Ultimate and Supreme God of All Creations.

I AM Love, the Cosmic Love of God.

I Feel the Cosmic Love of God within me. I Feel the Love of the Archangel Chamuel, Lady Charity and the Angels of Cosmic Love as they flood my Spirit, Soul, Mental/Emotional and Physical Body with their Unconditional Love and Compassion.

I Love myself Completely.
I AM Eternally Grateful to the Angelic Kingdom,
for bringing me back to the Pathway of Love.
From the Sacred Chambers of my Heart; I Transmit this Pathway of
Love out into the World. ".For this I Give Thanks and... So It Is!"

> Sacred Flame of Purification and Ascension – Image yourself
> within the vibrant Dazzling White Flame at the core center
> of the Sacred Flame and Ray of Purification and Ascension;
> Be in Acceptance of What Is, as Divine Perfection.

Ray 4: The White Ray,

The Sacred Flame of Purification and Ascension

Elohim: Purity and Astrea

Chohan: Lord Serapis Bey

Archangel: Gabriel

Divine Complement: Lady Hope

Key Attributes:

Ascended State of Self-Mastery-Wisdom, Peace and Tranquillity,

Acceptance, Balance, Harmony and Perfection of
Health, Christed Light Consciousness,

Self-Discipline and Access to Unlimited and Ever – present Supply
from The One, the Ultimate and Supreme God of All Creation.

Purification: Purity of Spirit, Mind and Body. Immortality: Of the Soul.

Sacred Flame Energy Amplified on Friday

Acceptance of what is, as Divine Perfection

Cosmic Ascension!

Prayer to the Chohan: Lord Serapis Bey, the Lord of Purification

Beloved Lord Serapis Bey, Lord of Purification, and the Beloved Ascension Brotherhood of Luxor, I AM here before you requesting, your guidance and assistance in my attainment of the Ascended State of Self-Mastery, Wisdom, Peace, Balance, Harmony, Perfect Health, Self-Discipline, and with Unlimited and Ever – present Supply.

I AM as you are, the Embodiment of Discipline on my Pathway of Ascension to the 5th Dimension and Beyond, to the many Dimensions of this Universe. I AM totally reliant upon my Mighty I AM Presence, the Lord God essence of my being within the Sacred Chambers of my Heart for the teachings and disciplines of the Ascension Brotherhood, which will allow me to shift my Conscious Awareness from outer – world concerns to the inner realms of my Heart Center, the seat of my Spiritual Divinity, the Sacred Chambers of my Heart, to my God-Self State, in order to manifest my Divine Spiritual Essence, my Mighty I AM Presence in physical manifestation.

I Call upon the white dazzling Sacred Ascension Flame and Ray of Purification and Immortality, to purify and transform all that is hindering my Transfiguration, Resurrection and Ascension into the arms of God's Unconditional Love; and the Restoration of all that I AM, of my Spiritual God-Self and the memories of All That Is.

I AM Resurrected, and Living as a Divine Child of The One, the Ultimate and Supreme God of All Creations, and Residing in the World of Christed Light of God Consciousness. I AM in Gratitude to you Lord Serapis Bey, and to the Ascension Brotherhood of Luxor, for your dedication in ensuring that I pass through the Fires of Purification and in supporting me to maintain Perseverance in my quest for Ascension, so that I AM indeed victorious.

I AM Transformed to Purity and Light in this now moment of time, And... So It Is!

Prayer of Gratitude and Release

Beloved One, the Ultimate and Supreme God of All Creations, my Mighty I AM Presence, Lord God essence of my Being. I AM your most humble servant. I AM pledged to serve you in any way that you desire. I AM here before you, with Open Heart and in Total Surrender to YOUR HEART, YOUR MIND and YOUR WILL.

I AM in Gratitude for All that I AM in this Life and All that I have been in all my Past Lives. I AM in Gratitude for All that I AM experiencing in this now moment that has come with me and been with me from my Past Life experiences to this very day. I AM in Gratitude for All the Knowledge, Wisdom and Understanding that I AM, because of the experiences of these lifetimes. I AM in Gratitude for ALL that I AM in this now moment of time. I AM in Gratitude for your Pledge to me of your Eternal Unconditional Love and Support, and that you are ever within me. I AM as you are; your Beloved Child. I AM in Gratitude for the Opportunity to RELEASE unto you, all that which is not of the Divine Spiritual Light and Love. I AM in Gratitude for the Lightbody that you have restored unto me Now!

I AM in Gratitude, Beloved One, the Ultimate and Supreme God of All Creations, for my RELEASE and FREEDOM from all the energies of spells, curses, implants, negative energies and blockages that had been placed upon me – in the present and in my past lives. I AM in Gratitude for my Freedom. I Release from my being all Beliefs associated with the Illusions of the Dark. I Accept the Illumine Truth of the Cosmic Christed Light of God Consciousness. I AM One with You. I AM Perfection, I AM All That Is!

I AM in Gratitude and I Thank You for your Faith in me and my Mighty I AM Presence. I AM in Gratitude for the Unconditional

Love of my Mighty I AM Presence and I AM in Gratitude for the
Unconditional Love that I AM I AM in Gratitude for my Spirit, Soul,
my Sacred Heart and I AM LOVE! I LOVE MYSELF COMPLETELY!
"And So It Is!"

Prayer for the Ascension of Planet Earth

I Call upon The Universal Hierarchy, the Universal Logos: Lord Melchizedek. The Planetary Logos: Lord Gautama Buddha. The Planetary Hierarchy: Lord Sanat Kumara and Lady Venus. The Planetary Christ: Lord Maitreya. The Lords of Karma; the Maha Chohan: Master St. Germain, and the Beloved Chohan: Lord Serapis Bey of the Sacred Flame and Ray of Ascension, Purification and Immortality, to be with me in this now moment of time.

I Desire the presence of Archangel Gabriel, the Divine Complement Lady Hope, and the dazzling White Angels of the Sacred Flame and Ray of Ascension. I Declare unto All the Kingdoms and Realms of Planet Earth at this time of great change, that I AM Awakened. I have come forth to request that the Light of a Thousand Suns aid Planet Earth in her Ascension to the 5th Dimension and beyond. I Decree that these changes occur with ease and grace for all concerned, and are for the Highest Good of Planet Earth, the entire Solar System and the Universe.

The Elohim: Purity and Astrea, and the Elohim Council of Elders ensure that all the criteria is met for the New Encodements of Planet Earth, as directed by the Cosmic Heart, Mind and Will of The One, Ultimate, Supreme God of All Creation.

I Decree that the magnificent dazzling white Sacred Flame and Ray of Ascension, Purification and Immortality, encapsulates, penetrates and infuses Planet Earth with the Divine Holy Spirit of Purity and Eternal Life, and elevates Planet Earth into her Spiritual Divinity and Ascension.

I Command that an Invincible Force Field of Protection encompasses, encapsulates and permeates Planet Earth. I Decree that this is done in accordance with the Divine Heart of God, the Mind of God and the Will of God, incorporating the Sacred Flames and Rays of Cosmic Love, Illumination and Wisdom, and the Will of God – which are Three-Fold Flames from the Cosmic Heart of God. I AM In Gratitude and Love for Planet Earth's Ascension. "And... So It Is!"

Prayer for Personal Ascension

Beloved Lord Serapis Bey, Lord of Love, the Ascension Brotherhood, the Office of the Christed Light of God Consciousness, Archangel Gabriel and the Divine Complement Lady Hope and the Ascension Angels from the Temple of Ascension.

I Desire from the Sacred Chambers of my Heart for the Grace of Ascension in this incarnation. I AM dedicated to be firm and vigilant in my commitment to my Cosmic Ascension, until that Glorious Victory becomes my Reality.

I Have Your Guidance and Support, as I Let Go of the Lower Dimensional Consciousness of separation, duality, polarity and drama, in all its many guises and forms. I Let Go of Judgements and Expectations about myself and others, and in how life should unfold for me.

I Have Fully embraced my Holy Vows – the Holy Vows that are held within my cellular memory, cellular structure and DNA, and also found residing in the Sacred Chambers of my Heart. I AM Conscious and I AM Connected and United in Oneness with my Mighty I AM Presence. I AM Totally Determined to fulfil the Divine Plan for my life – the Ascension, Unification and Merger into the magnificence that is my Mighty I AM Presence.

I AM Love, harmlessness and the truth of my Spiritual Divinity. I AM the Consciousness of Harmony. I honor the sanctity of all life and All the Kingdoms and Realms sharing Planet Earth with me. I AM Living from my Heart, talking and behaving like an Ascended Master as a way of being in the world. The Master that I AM is Awake and Alert. I Recognize the Master within my Heart as my Mighty I AM Presence.

I Release and Relinquish into the Sacred Fires of Purification all old beliefs, patterns and programs, all negative emotions stored in my conscious, unconscious, and super-consciousness memories, including all the beliefs about the balancing of all karmic debts incurred toward life.

I AM the Attitude of Love for All of Humanity, for Mother Earth and All the Kingdoms and Realms of Earth. I AM in the Attitude of Gratitude for All of Creation and for All that I AM. I AM in Gratitude and Give Thanks to Lord Serapis Bey, to the Ascension Brotherhood of Luxor, to Archangel Gabriel, and the Divine Complement Lady Hope, and the Ascension Flame Angels. For all your guidance, love and support for my heartfelt desire for my Ascension to Immortality in this Lifetime.

Beloved I AM! "And... So It Is!"

Prayer at the Portal of Cosmic Ascension

Beloved One, the Ultimate and Supreme God of All Creations, Beloved Elohim: Co-Creator Gods. The Cosmic Logos: the Avatar of Synthesis: the Mahatma. The Universal Logos: Lord Melchizedek; and the Universal Hierarchy; Beloved Planetary Logos: Lord Gautama Buddha; and the Planetary Hierarchy: Lord Sanat Kumara, Lady Venus and Lord Zohar of Shamballa. Beloved Planetary Christ: Lord Maitreya. The Maha Chohan: St. Germain and the Chohans of the Twelve Sacred Flames and Rays of Christed Light of God Consciousness.

Lord Metatron; the Archangels and their Divine Complements, and the Planetary Ascension Council of Luxor: Lord Sanat Kumara, Lord Serapis Bey and Lord Sananda.

My Beloved Overself, my Mighty I AM Presence, Lord God essence of my Being, I AM that I AM. I Stand before you this day, the day of my Cosmic Ascension to the 5th Dimension and Beyond. I AM Purified by the Sacred Flame and Ray of Ascension, and Initiated to all levels in all the Temples of the Sacred Flames and Rays. I Meet All the Requirements to make my Cosmic Ascension on this day to higher levels of consciousness.

I AM Humbled by this Honor. I feel deep Gratitude for what is to take place. I AM that I AM.

I Choose to be of Service to Humanity and Planet Earth, if that be in accordance with the Divine Plan for my Incarnation and Cosmic Ascension.

I AM ALL THAT I AM, I AM ALL THAT IS!

I Surrender and Release ALL energies, vibrations and frequencies that are within my entire beingness, to the Purification of the Cosmic Ascension process. My Crystalline Lightbody is Anchored, Activated,

Actualized and Amplified within my being, bringing me to Optimum Health, Oneness and Unity Consciousness.

I Believe that All is in Accordance with what The One, the Ultimate and Supreme God of All Creations Decrees. I Desire to Live my Life in Accordance with the Decrees of The One, the Ultimate and Supreme God of All Creations.

God's Cosmic Heart, Mind and Will comprise the Cosmic Laws of One Unity Consciousness.

Thy Will Is Done, Thy Will Is Done, Thy Will Is Done, Now!
GOD IS WITHIN ME – I AM ALL THAT IS!
"And... So It Is!"

Prayer for Immortality

I Manifest the Cosmic Blueprint of the whole-brain experience in this now moment of time and space, with the vibrations and frequencies of my Mighty I AM Presence.

I AM made whole again and I AM immortal.

I Breathe in the Sound Wave Frequency that communicates with my Body Elemental, to assist my body to an Anti-aging, Balanced God-Self State of Immortality.

I Breathe into my body from the ether and the atmosphere the elements, vibrational waves and frequencies that will promote Longevity and expand my Spirituality.

I AM Healthy. My flow of Chi Energy and my perfect diet enhance my lifestream and mobility. My third eye is activated by the wondrous vibrations and frequencies of my Mighty I AM Presence.

I AM Spiritually Aligned with the Masculine and Feminine Energies contained within my body. I AM Balanced and Harmonized on all levels of my being, My Spirit, Soul, Heart, Mind, Emotion, Body and Body Elemental are the Embodiment of The One, the Ultimate and Supreme God of All Creations.

I AM Living in my Heart, the Heart of Inner Peace, Total Surrender and Unconditional Love.

Immortal and Infinite I AM! "And... So It Is!"

Prayer for the Purification of Mind, Body, Spirit and Soul

I Call upon Lord Serapis Bey to aid me in my Journey, bringing to me the Purification of my Mind, Body, Spirit and Soul. With this Purification I move forward and manifest for myself greater discipline in my life, on all levels of my beingness. Also, for me to be ready for Ascension, and thereby be of greater service to Humanity, Mother Earth and All the Kingdoms and Realms of Planer Earth.

I Hereby Surrender all resistance that is part of me to my Mighty I AM Presence and to the Sacred Flame and Ray of Ascension, Purification and Immortality, receiving in return all the Healing that I require.

I AM my Mighty I AM Presence and I State that I AM willing to Release all negative energy within my being, and from all levels of my being, my Spiritual, Soul, Mental, Emotional, Body Elemental, Inner Child and all Subtle Energy Bodies – to bring in the effects of Purity and the Divine Perfection of Health to my Mind, Body, Spirit and Soul.

I Thank You and Accept this as being done for my Highest Good and the Highest Good of All, in accordance with the Divine Will and the Divine Perfection of The One, the Ultimate and Supreme God of All Creations. The All That Is!

"And... So It Is!"

Invocation to the Elohim: Purity and Astrea for Purification

Beloved Elohim: Purity and Astrea of the Sacred Flame and Ray of Ascension, Purification and Immortality. I Invoke the Godforce Energy of the Elohim Purity and Astrea into my lifestream for this incarnation.

I Desire the Purification and Discipline necessary for my Ascension to the 5th Dimension and beyond. I Hereby Ask and I Humbly Pray with all of my Sacred Heart, Mind, Spirit, Soul and Might – to have the Purity of Heart, Mind, Body, Spirit and Soul, that I am able to see my Mighty I AM Presence and Holy God-Self.

I Desire with all of my being to purify all my past negative human creations, and to transform them to pure-white dazzling light radiance.

I Command that the energy manifested from this invocation be woven into a spiral of Purity and Ascension energy, the gathering of which will lead to a greater cosmic momentum of energy going up to Source, the All That Is!

I Thank you for your blessings and Accept this as being done according to the Divine Will in the Divine Perfection of The One, the Ultimate and Supreme God of All Creations. The All That Is!

I AM That I AM! "And... So It Is!"

Prayer to the Archangel Gabriel and the Divine Complement Lady Hope

Beloved Archangel Gabriel and Lady Hope, in all the days of my incarnations, I have Desired from the depths of my Spirit and Soul to Ascend to higher levels of Christed Light of God Consciousness. To Ascend to the 5th Dimension and Beyond, and transcend the need to reincarnate into lifestreams, in which I have endured the pain of separation from The One, the Ultimate and Supreme God of All Creations, the All That Is.

In this Journey, I have been lost and I have been in pain and torment. From my Spirit and Soul, I Reach out to find the Keys to Inner Peace, Purity and Immortality, and to be made whole again, healed and ready to return to the Truth of Who I AM.

I Hold a Memory of a place that is all of Inner Peace, Purity and Immortality, a memory of a time when I knew the Truth of Who I AM.

I AM this day Releasing to the Sacred Flame and Ray of Ascension, and to the Ascension Flame Angels all that which is within me that requires purification.

I Release it all so that I AM Free, Purified on all levels of my being, and made ready to receive All the Initiations required for my Ascension to the 5th Dimension and beyond. Wisdom and Understanding comes to me with ease and grace.

I AM in Gratitude to the Archangel Gabriel and the Divine Complement Lady Hope for keeping the Sacred Flame and Ray of Ascension, Purification and Immortality alive in my Heart and the Memory of Home within my Mind, Body, Spirit and Soul. I Remember the Truth of Who I AM. I AM Living from my Heart. I AM One with myself, others and The One, the Ultimate and Supreme God of All Creation, the All That Is!

"I AM Forever Grateful, And... So It Is!"

Prayer to the Angels of Ascension and Purification

Beloved Archangel Gabriel, the Divine Complement Lady Hope and All the Angels of Ascension and Purification; As I Accept myself and the Truth of who I AM, a much Loved Child of God, I Feel your Presence and I Know you are within me, encompassing every level of my being with the Purification of the white dazzling Light of Ascension.

I AM Purified and I AM Disciplined. I Receive from you the Knowledge of Purification and Discipline and because I have this Knowledge, I AM able to Discipline my Mental/Emotional and Physical Body, to persevere in the Ascension and Purification processes necessary, for my Initiations in all the required levels, and thereby gain Acceptance into the Halls of Ascension.

In my Victory of Ascension to the 5th Dimension and Beyond, I Give Thanks to Archangel Gabriel, Lady Hope and All the Angels of Ascension and Purification.

I Acknowledge that my Ascension to the 5th Dimension and Beyond during my Physical Incarnation, facilitates the Physical Ascension of Planet Earth for her Ascension to the 5th Dimension.

I AM Eternally Grateful for having achieved my Self-Mastery, Inner Peace and Tranquillity.

I Give Thanks to Archangel Gabriel, Lady Hope and All the Angels of Ascension and Purification, for teaching me Purity, Self-Discipline and the processes necessary for my Ascension.

I AM in Gratitude for the Feelings of Hope that you Inspired within me to achieve my Ascension.

Beloved I AM! "And... So It Is!"

> Sacred Emerald Flame of Healing and Manifestation – Image yourself within the Living Life energy the Green Flame at the core center of the Sacred Emerald Flame and Ray of Healing and Manifestation. Connect with the Healing and Manifestation energy of your Mighty I AM Presence.

Ray 5: The Green Ray,

The Sacred Emerald Flame of Healing and Manifestation

Elohim: Cyclopea and Virginia

Chohan: Master Hilarion

Archangel: Raphael

Divine Complement: Lady Regina

Key Attributes:

Divine Healing of Physical Pain and Dis-ease, Poverty Thinking, Mental/Emotional Confusion, Critical Thinking about Self and Others, Healing at All Levels, Constancy, Creation through Manifestation, God's Abundance through the Immaculate Sacred Heart of I AM.

Sacred Flame Energy Amplified on Wednesday

Divine Abundance of Perfect Health in Mind, Body and Soul

The Divine Healing Power of God!

Prayer to the Chohan: Master Hilarion for Guidance

I Call upon Beloved Master Hilarion, all the Masters and Lady Masters of the Sacred Emerald Flame and Ray of Healing and Manifestation.

I Request of you in this period of my life, your guidance – to counsel and guide me in the ways best suited for me to achieve the Healing of my Physical, Mental and Emotional Being, on all levels of my Auric Fields. So that my body is free and full of the Divine Healing Power of the Sacred Flame and Ray of Healing.

I Desire your Wisdom and Understanding so that I too may be as you are, and walk as you walk, in Perfect Health, Balance and Harmony in every now moment.

I Desire from my Heart and Mind to talk as you talk in all manner of communication; that I Express myself in the ways that you express yourselves, in that like you, my Mind, Emotions and Heart will be free and full of the Divine Abundance of Perfect Health in Mind, Body, Spirit and Soul.

I AM living my Life in service to the Divine Holy Spirit of the All That Is, in accordance with the desires of my Beloved Mighty I AM Presence.

I Invoke the Laws of Manifestation that the life I lead during this incarnation is a Life of Total Abundance in Prosperity, Health and with Loving, Harmonious Relationships. I Believe that all that which is made manifest in my Life is for my Highest Good and the Highest Good of All.

For this I AM Grateful. "And... So It Is!"

Prayer for Health and Wellbeing

Beloved Chohan: Master Hilarion of the Sacred Flame and Ray of Healing and Manifestation. Beloved Masters and Lady Masters of the Sacred Flame and Ray and the Beloved Archangel: Raphael and the Divine Complement Lady Regina, and the Green Ray Angels of the Sacred Flame and Ray of Healing and Manifestation.

My Beloved Mighty I AM Presence, Lord God essence of my being. My entire being – my Spirit, Soul, Mental, Emotional, Physical Body and Elemental Body, are encapsulated and immersed within waves upon waves of the Sacred Emerald Flames of Healing.

I AM received at the Great Jade Temple of Healing, my Health and Wellbeing are Restored to the Divine Perfection of Eternal Youth and Beauty.

I AM Rejuvenated and Revivified to the Optimum Healing that I AM able to attain; sustain and maintain at this point in time.

I Know these Healing Procedures are for my Highest Good and for the Highest Good of All, and take place when I AM asleep, resting and relaxed.

I AM Grateful – I Give Thanks to all those concerned in my Healing Procedures.

Perfection in Health I AM! "And... So It Is!"

Prayer for the Abundance of God

Beloved One, the Ultimate and Supreme God of All Creations, the All That Is,

I AM that I AM, and in the name of my Beloved Mighty I AM Presence, and the Beloved Holy Spirit that I AM, I AM my Sacred Heart. I Call upon the Lords of Manifestation, the Angels of Prosperity, Goddess Fortuna and the Lord of Gold.

I AM my Sacred Heart. I Call upon the Holy Spirit of the Great White Brotherhood, to Release Abundance of Wealth from your Unlimited Supply of Prosperity to me Now!

I AM my Mighty I AM Presence. I AM manifesting a continuous Flow of Wealth, in order to become the Divine Perfection required to manifest my Life Plan, in this now moment of time.

I AM my Mighty I AM Presence, directing and manifesting Great Abundance, including all the Prosperity of Money that I will ever need, from The One, the Ultimate and Supreme God of All Creations, the All That Is.

I Praise God. In the Silence of my Heart and Mind, within the Sacred Chambers of my Heart, I AM in Gratitude that I have it Now! As I speak these words from the Silence that is Golden, my prayers are manifested and I AM Prosperity.

Prosperity I AM! "And So It Is!"

Prayer for the Waters of the World

Beloved Elohim: Cyclopea and Virginia of the 5th Ray, the Sacred Flame and Ray of Healing and Manifestation Master Hilarion, the Beloved Chohan, of the Sacred Flame and Ray of Healing and Manifestation, Archangel Raphael and the Divine Complement Lady Regina, All Masters and Lady Masters of the Great Jade Temple of the Sacred Flame and Ray of Healing and Manifestation. And my Beloved Mighty I AM Presence Lord God essence of my being,

I Invoke the Sacred Flame of Healing to come forth and Heal the Waters of the World. I Invoke the Sacred Flame of Healing to come forth and Heal the Waters of the World. I Invoke the Sacred Flame of Healing to come forth and Heal the Waters of the World.
I Invoke the Light of God within, I am a Clear and Perfect Channel, Light is my guide. I Invoke the Light of God within, I am a Clear and Perfect Channel, Light is my guide. I Invoke the Light of God within, I am a Clear and Perfect Channel, Light is my guide.

Master Hilarion, the Chohan of the Sacred Flame and Ray of Healing and Manifestation; Transmits from the Great Jade Temple of Healing and Manifestation the Sacred Healing energies to the Waters of the World – the Oceans, Seas, Bays, Rivers and Streams – and for all the living creatures that live in these areas, that they be cleansed and purified of all that is not of the Divine Light and Love of the Cosmic Christed Light of God Consciousness.

The Elohim: of the 5th Ray; Cyclopea and Virginia, activate and actualize the Sacred Flame and Ray of Healing, to saturate the Waterways of Planet Earth with Waves upon Waves of the Sacred Flame and Ray

Healing Energy, to Cleanse and Restore them to Purity and Divine Optimum Health.

The Lords of Manifestation and the Guardians of Planet Earth, amplify the energies of the Sacred Flame and Ray of Healing, and send these Healing energies to: The Whales, Dolphins, Pelicans, Fish, Shellfish, Planktons, Coral Life Forms, and to the Algae and all living creatures that dwell in the waters of the world.

I AM in Deepest Gratitude to the Waters of the World for the life that they bring unto me. I Honor the Mighty Elohim: Cyclopea and Virginia, with all of my being for their Cosmic Presence. I Give thanks to Master Hilarion and all the Masters and Lady Masters for the Sacred Flame and Ray of Healing and Manifestation.

I AM in Gratitude and I Rejoice in the Presence of Archangel Raphael and the Divine Complement Lady Regina. Blessings to you All; Thank You, Beloved All That Is!

"And... So It Is!"

Prayer for Healing and Cosmic Ascension

I AM that I AM. I Call upon Beloved Master Hilarion, the Masters and Lady Masters of the Sacred Flame and Ray of Healing, the Archangel Raphael and the Divine Complement Lady Regina and my Beloved Mighty I AM Presence.

Receive from me all the negative energies held within my Spirit, Soul, my four Body Systems and All Subtle Bodies. And transform these negative energies into positive energies, bringing to me Balance, Harmony and Perfect Health.

I Affirm that All patterns and programs that are still held within my Spirit, Soul, my four Body Systems and All Subtle Bodies, have been transmuted and transformed to resourceful beliefs and positive concepts in this now moment of time.

From which I have gained the Wisdom and Understanding of these beliefs, patterns and programs that have thus enhanced and achieved my Healing on all levels of my being and promoted my Cosmic Ascension to the 5th Dimension and beyond.

I AM in Deepest Gratitude to The One, the Ultimate and Supreme God of All Creations, the All That Is, and our Beloved Mother Earth.

"And... So It Is!"

Prayer of the Emerald Fire

I AM Prayer

I AM the Vibration of the Sacred Emerald Fire. As I breathe in, I take within me the vibrant alchemy that blends my Heart and Grail Energies with the powerful frequencies and waves of fire that are radiating through my Heart Chakra from my Divine Realms of Loving Intention and Wholeness.

I AM the Exquisite Soundwaves of Frequency that are of flowing Heart Healing, helping me to be in alignment with my Heart Wisdom and encouraging my Higher Self Purpose of centeredness, emotional balance and courageous, compassionate living my Life Core.

I AM the Power of this Sacred Emerald Flame as it is packed with Love, opening my Heart to the Universal Grace, the Holy Grail.

I AM the Loving Vibrations that radiate love, inner peace, wealth and abundance. I AM the strong Spiritual "Heart Medicine" that helps my physical heart and emotional body to be in balance and hold the feelings of worthiness.

I AM the Emerald Fire Flaming in my Heart.
I AM That I AM! "And... So It Is!"

Prayer for Personal Prosperity

Beloved Sacred Flame and Ray of Prosperity: Lords of Manifestation and Fortuna – Goddess of Wealth. I Anchor, Activate, Actualized and Amplify from within the Sacred Chambers of my Heart, the Keys of Prosperity, in order to be of Greater Service to The One, the Ultimate and Supreme God of All Creations, and that this also is for my Highest Good and the Highest Good of the Universe.

I AM All That Is, I AM Totally Wealthy, Healthy and Happy in my Life.

I AM Thankful and in Total Gratitude for ALL
the Prosperity that I AM in my Life.
I AM Open to receive the Abundance of my Mighty
I AM Presence in all areas of my life.
I AM Rich in all areas of my Life. I Hold within me the
Keys to the Prosperity of the Creator, The One, Ultimate
and Supreme God of All Creations, the All That Is.

Thy Will Is Done, Thy Will Is Done, Thy Will Is Done!
Divine Prosperity I AM! "And… So It Is!"

Invocation to Elohim: Cyclopea and Virginia for Healing

I Invoke the Godforce Energy of the Elohim: Cyclopea and Virginia of the 5th Ray, the Sacred Flame and Ray of Healing, to Anchor and Activate the Cosmic Rays of Healing for Humanity, and All the Kingdoms and Realms of Planet Earth.

Humanity and All the Kingdoms and Realms of Planet Earth are now Cleansed and Restored to Purity and Divine Perfection of Health.

I Hereby Invoke Divine Intervention into all the affairs of World Governments and Corporations that have a direct impact on the Health and Well-being of Planet Earth, its environment and all of the inhabitance of Planet Earth.

I AM in Gratitude to the Elohim: Cyclopea and Virginia, for all that you do.

I Thank You and Accept this as being done according to the Divine Will in the Divine Perfection of All That Is.

I Hereby Ask and Humbly pray with all of my Sacred Heart, Spirit, Soul, Mind and Might that all is done with ease and grace, and for the Highest Good of Humanity, All the Kingdoms and Realms of Planet Earth, the Solar System and this Universe.

Divine Perfection and Restoration to Christed Light of God Consciousness is happening Now!

"And… So It Is!"

Prayer to Archangel Raphael and the Divine Complement Lady Regina

Beloved Archangel Raphael and the Divine Complement Lady Regina, I AM in Gratitude for the Healing that I AM receiving from you in this now moment of time. I Ask for Healing and Guidance regarding the Cause of my Physical, Mental and Emotional Pain, so that I AM able to Heal and Purify the many levels of my being that are in need of healing, through the Wisdom and Understanding of the Negative Causes, that are creating the Negative Effects in my Life.

I Desire counselling from you and the Angelic Realm in the many ways of healing all my beliefs, patterns and programs that have caused and kept me in pain. I AM prepared to be guided by you in the manifestation of my Abundance in Health and Wellness, for all the levels of my four Body Systems, my Spirit, Soul, Body Elemental and Inner Child.

I Accept that All is Divine Perfection and I Know I AM ready to be the truth of Who I AM, I Desire from my Heart to clear and cleanse the Veils of Forgetfulness, and to Release to the Emerald Angels of Healing All that which serves me not. All the negative energy that had been attached to me at any and all levels, is now transformed by the magnificence of the Emerald Green Fire to the manifestations of Abundance in Health, Prosperity and Loving, Caring Relationships with Myself, Others and the Universe.

I Give Thanks to you, Archangel Raphael and Lady Regina. I Know that all will be done with Divine ease and grace.

In the Acceptance from my Heart of my Pain, I See it and accept it as; it is what it is, Divine Perfection.

I AM therefore Free of my pain. "And... So It Is!"

Sacred Flame of Resurrection and Immortality – Image yourself within the Vibrant energy of the Ruby/Golden Flame, at the core center of the Sacred Flame and Ray of Resurrection and Immortality, in Selfless Service, Ministration and One Unity Consciousness.

Ray 6: The Ruby/Golden Ray,

The Sacred Flame of Resurrection and Immortality

Elohim: Peace and Aloha

Chohan: Lord Sananda

Archangel: Uriel

Divine Complement: Lady Aurora

Key Attributes:

Immortality, Mortality, Perfectionism, Planetary Service, and Time Related issues, Resurrection, Restoration, Revivification, Regeneration to the New Encodements of Divine Perfection and Spiritual Worship and Reverence.

Sacred Flame Energy Amplified on Thursday

Selfless Service and Ministration

The Resurrection to Immortality!

Prayer to Chohan: Lord Sananda, for the Resurrection of My Life

Beloved Lord Sananda, in Reverence to you and the Eternal Sacred Flame and Ray of Resurrection, I Decree that I AM as you are in Service and Ministration to The One, the Ultimate and Supreme God of All Creations.

In my Spiritual True God-Self State, I AM That I AM:

I AM That I AM, I AM my Higher Self. I AM That I AM, I AM my Mighty I AM Presence. I AM That I AM, I AM my Spiritual Divinity, I AM One with All Creation.

I AM the Resurrection of my Life; I AM Rejuvenated and Restored to the New Encodements of Divine Perfection.

I AM the Resurrection of my Life; I AM Healed Completely of All Pain and Trauma.

I AM the Resurrection of my Life; I AM Living in the Now! I AM the Resurrection of my Life; I AM Living in the Unconditional Love and Light of the Cosmic Love and Light of Source, the All That Is.

I AM the Resurrection of my Life; I AM a Christed Light of God Consciousness Spiritual Soul. I AM the Resurrection of my Life; I AM in my Ascension to the 5th Dimension and Beyond.

I AM the Resurrection of my Life; I AM in Oneness and Unity, with The One, the Ultimate and Supreme God of All Creations, the ALL That Is.

Resurrected to Oneness I AM! "And... So It Is!"

Prayer to the Sacred Flame and Ray of Resurrection

I Call upon the Sacred Flame and Ray of Resurrection to enter my Physical Heart and lifestream, and Restore my Spirit, my Soul, my Heart, and my four Body Systems to the normal, natural Spiritual God-Self State of Divine Perfection and Immortality.

I Decree that I AM the Resurrection of my Life.

I AM the Resurrection of my Lightbody in this now moment of time and space.

I AM the Resurrection of the New Encodements of Divine Perfection.

I AM the Resurrection of my True God-Self State. As an infinite being of God Consciousness my entire consciousness, being and world are immersed within this wondrous Sacred Flame and Ray of Resurrection. I AM the Embodiment of Selfless Service and Ministration to the All That Is. Thy Will is done on Earth Now, as it is in Heaven, in Accordance with the Divine Heart, Mind and Will of The One, the All That Is.

The Sacred Flame and Ray of Resurrection Blesses All with Eternal Life!
"And... So It Is!"

Invocation to the Sacred Flame and Ray of Resurrection

Beloved Mother/Father God, Beloved Lord Sananda, Chohan of the Sacred Flame and Ray of Resurrection, and my Beloved Mighty I AM Presence, Lord God essence of my being.

I Invoke the Power of the Sacred Flame and Ray of Resurrection to revivify my body, mind, emotions and affairs.

I AM free in its Revivifying Life-Giving essence. I Call upon the Restorative and Revivifying Life-Giving essence of the Resurrection Flame and Ray to Restore me to Optimum Health and Well-being.

I AM the Resurrection of my Life, I AM the Resurrection of my Life, I AM the Resurrection of my Life. The Resurrection Flame and Ray Restore my mind, emotions, body and world to its rightful True God-Self State.

I AM my True God-Self State Now! I Embody the Resurrection Flame and Ray. I Accept that I AM the Perfection of Eternal Youth, Beauty and Immortality.

I AM the Resurrection Flame and Ray Now! Resurrected I AM to Immortality.

"And... So It Is!"

Prayer for the Resurrection of Planet Earth

Beloved Lord Sananda, Chohan of the Sacred Flame and Ray of Resurrection, and the Beloved Archangel Uriel and the Divine Complement Lady Aurora.

I Invoke the Sacred Flame and Ray of Resurrection, to send waves upon waves of wondrous Ruby/Golden Fire Energy to surround Planet Earth in a Golden Halo of Christed Light – that will restore this beautiful Planet to her True God-Self State of Perfection. And to prepare her to receive the full Transformation of the Ascension Flame and Ray, and the energies that will assist her in moving into the 5th Dimension and beyond.

I Decree that the Sacred Flame and Ray of Resurrection has Purified the Electrons of Planet Earth which have been misused and restored them to Health, Harmony and Tranquillity.

I Invoke the Sacred Flame and Ray of Resurrection to Restore and Rejuvenate Planet Earth to Harmony and Peace, healing all issues that caused the separation of Humanity from their True God-Self State, and so bring to all, the Oneness and Unity Consciousness of The One, the Ultimate and Supreme God of All Creations, the All That Is.

In this now moment of time, Thy Will Is Done, Thy Will Is Done, Thy Will Is Done.

Beloved We Are! "And... So It Is!"

Prayer: Born to Be in this Moment of Time

In this Moment, it is Time to Resurrect the Truth of All That I AM.

In this Moment, it is Time to Resurrect the Purpose of All That I AM.

In this Moment, it is Time to Resurrect the Life of All That I AM.

In this Moment, it is Time to Resurrect the Light of All That I AM.

In this Moment, it is Time to Resurrect the Love of All That I AM.

In this moment, it is Time to Resurrect the I AM of All That I AM.

It is Time, my Beloved Mighty I AM Presence, for the Resurrection of
my Dream to Live the Life I AM Born to Live, to Resurrect my Purpose
and Be it in the Life I AM Born to Be in, to Resurrect my Lightbody
and Bring it into the Life I AM born to Bring it in and to Resurrect
my Immortality and Enter into the Life I AM Born to Enter as I AM.

I AM the Resurrection of my Life, I AM the Resurrection
of my Life, I AM the Resurrection of my Life.

I Live in, I Be in, I Bring in and I Enter as I AM, my Lightbody
and the Oneness of Christed Light of God Consciousness.

In this Moment, It Is Time Now!

"And... So It Is!"

Prayer for Restoration and Healing

Beloved Lord Sananda and the Beloved Angels and Masters of the Sacred Flame and Ray of Resurrection and my Beloved Mighty I AM Presence, Lord God essence of my being, the Sacred Flame and Ray of Resurrection purify and restore the electrons of my four Body Systems back to Health, Balance and Harmony.

I Invoke the Sacred Flame and Ray of Resurrection to restore Harmony into my Life, and to heal all issues that cause me to be in separation from my True Divine God-Self. I Desire to be in the Oneness and Unity of the Christed Light of God Consciousness.

The Sacred Flame and Ray of Resurrection cleanse and raise my vibrations and frequencies in all my four Body Systems, to the vibrations and frequencies that are the Divine Perfection of my True God-Self State.

All the Experiences I have in my Life are God's Will and are for my Highest Good and the Highest Good of All. Perfect Health and Harmony I AM!

"And... So It Is!"

Prayer for the Resurrection of My Body Elemental

Beloved Lord Sananda, Chohan of the Sacred Flame and Ray of Resurrection. Beloved Archangel Uriel and the Divine Complement Lady Aurora, and the Angels of the Resurrection Flame. The Beloved Elementals of Nature and my Beloved Mighty I AM Presence.

I Call upon your aid and the Sacred Flame and Ray of Resurrection to restore the health, vitality and the energy of immortality to my Body Elemental.

I Desire for my Body Elemental to release all energies about my past neglect and embrace the Resurrection Fires of Rejuvenation which will Restore and Revivify my Body Elemental to Optimum Well-being and to the Divine Perfection of Immortality.

I AM in Gratitude to my Body Elemental for having been with me throughout my experience in the lower dimensions.

I Ask my Body Elemental to be with me as we enter the higher dimensions of Christed Light of God Consciousness, and to embrace the frequencies and vibrations of the Lightbody of the Christed Light as it comes into my being with the Sacred Flame and Ray of Resurrection, and for this to occur with ease, grace and acceptance.

My Body Elemental and I are One! "And… So It Is!"

Prayer for the Resurrection of the Elemental Kingdom

I Call upon the Beloved Elemental Kingdom, Beloved Mother, Goddess of Earth and All the Kingdoms and Realms of Earth.

I Request your forgiveness for all the damage that you have endured, for all that has happened to you during Humanity's sojourn here on Planet Earth, as part of the experiment of being incarnated into the lower consciousness, vibrations and frequencies of the 3rd Dimension.

Without your assistance in this experiment, the experiences that have been endured by Humanity and All the Kingdoms and Realms of Earth, for their evolution and the evolution of the Universe, could not have occurred.

I Ask you to accept my Heartfelt Gratitude for all that you have experienced and have done throughout these eons of time to keep our Beloved Mother, Goddess of Earth, alive and in wellness.

I Acknowledge the Elemental Kingdom, for everything that you have accomplished in keeping alive all of Nature, the Elements of Earth, Air, Fire and Water. I AM in Awe of what you have achieved. Because of your Dedication and Service to the Beloved Mother, Goddess of Earth and to Father/Mother God of Creation, All the Kingdoms and Realms of Planet Earth are still here to evolve, to be in Oneness and Unity of All That Is.

I Stand in Reverence of all that you have accomplished. I Love all that you are and what you have achieved and I Thank Lord Sananda, the Chohan of the Sacred Flame and Ray of Resurrection for his Resurrection to Eternal Life, for showing the way back home to Immortality through the Fires of the Sacred Flame and Ray of Resurrection.

Because of your dedication and all that you represent, I Know that I too can be as you and return to be in the Oneness and Unity Consciousness of All That Is.

I Ask that the Sacred Flame and Ray of Resurrection surround Planet Earth, All the Elementals and All the Kingdoms and Realms of Earth with waves upon waves of the Sacred Flame and Ray of Resurrection and thereby Rejuvenate, Regenerate and Restore Planet Earth and All the Kingdoms and Realms of Planet Earth to the New Encodements of Divine Perfection in the Oneness of the Christed Light of God Consciousness.

"And… So It Is!"

Invocation to the Elohim: Peace and Aloha for Resurrection

Aloha! Beloved Elohim: Peace and Aloha. Blessings to you at your retreat in the Hawaiian Islands of Planet Earth,

I Invoke the Energy of Peace and Aloha into the World. I Reach out to you in Honor and Gratitude for your Presence here on Planet Earth, and as you raise up the Sacred Resurrection Flame and Ray of Light and Love, to Swamp this world with Waves upon Waves of the Resurrection Flame and Ray – you Resurrect the Life of the Eternal Energy of Peace, Tranquillity and Harmony into this World for the Highest Good of Humanity, and All the Kingdoms and Realms of Planet Earth.

The Resurrection of the Aloha Energy gathers up the Hearts of Humanity and Propels them forward to Unconditional Love of Self and Others, with Compassion and Charity toward all of Humanity and All the Kingdoms and Realms of Earth; the Animal Kingdom, the Mineral Kingdom, the Fairy Kingdoms, the Plant and Tree Kingdoms and All Other Kingdoms and Realms that share this wonderful world upon which we live.

All of their combined energies Reach out to meet with you in the Resurrection of Aloha and Peace for Planet Earth.

Aloha! And Mahalo! To you, Beloved Elohim: Peace and Aloha!
"And So It Is!

Prayer to Archangel Uriel and the Divine Complement Lady Aurora

I Call upon the Beloved Archangel Uriel and the Divine Complement Lady Aurora. Greetings to you and Thank You for all that you are and have been for the Christed Light of God Consciousness in the World and for Planet Earth.

I AM in Gratitude to the Sacred Flame and Ray of Resurrection for the Life Changes that they bring forth for me from the Sacred Chambers of my Heart.

I Believe in the Powers of the Sacred Flame and Ray of Resurrection. I Feel the influence of the Resurrection Angels in all areas of my Life. The Resurrection of my Life is in the Acceptance of the Sacred Flame and Ray of Resurrection and the Resurrection Angels – as my Life is changed, Resurrected, Restored and Rejuvenated, in accordance to my Heart's Desire and the Divine Plan for my Life in this incarnation.

I AM the Resurrection of my Life, I AM the Resurrection
of my Life, I AM the Resurrection of my Life of Oneness
with the Archangel Uriel and Lady Aurora.

I Give Thanks for your Presence in the World and for All that you do, for the Resurrection of Humanity to Eternal Life, and the Resurrection of Planet Earth to the 5th Dimension and the Resurrection of the Christed Light of God Consciousness of The One, the Ultimate and Supreme God of All Creation, the All That Is.

Resurrected to Eternal Life I AM!
"And... So It Is!"

The Sacred Flame of Transmutation and Freedom – Image yourself within a Circle of Violet Fire, at the central core of the Violet Flame of The Sacred Flame of Transmutation, Feel the Energy of Freedom, Forgiveness and Unconditional Love.

Ray 7: The Violet Ray

The Sacred Flame of Transmutation and Freedom

Elohim: Arcturus and Victoria

Chohan: Lady Portia

Archangel: Zadkiel

Divine Complement: Lady Amethyst

Key Attributes:

Transmutation: to Freedom, Forgiveness and Unconditional Love. Transformation: Change, Acceptance of God's Will, Tact and Diplomacy. Ceremony and the Application of the Science of True Alchemy;

Sacred Flame Energy Amplified on Saturday.

Transmutation to Freedom, Forgiveness and Unconditional Love –

Violet Flame of Omri Tas from The Violet Planet!

Prayer to Chohan: Lady Portia for Justice and Opportunity

Beloved Lady Portia, Goddess of Justice and Opportunity, Chohan of the Sacred Violet Flame and Ray of Transmutation, Freedom and Forgiveness. Beloved Master St. Germain, Beloved Archangel Zadkiel and the Divine Complement Lady Amethyst, and the Violet Flame Angels from the Great Violet Flame Temple.

Beloved Masters and Lady Masters of the Violet Flame and Ray, in the name and authority of my Beloved Mighty I AM Presence, I Come before you in humbleness and gratitude. I Thank You for holding the vibration and frequency of the 7th Ray, the Sacred Violet Flame of Transmutation.

I AM seeking the way to Justice and Freedom of Opportunity, for all levels of my being. I Desire from my Heart to be Just and Fair, Merciful, Compassionate and Caring toward myself and others. I Ask for your guidance, Lady Portia, in delivering unto myself True Acceptance and Forgiveness that comes from my Heart of All-Knowing, so that I completely understand myself and my fellow Humanity, and thereby I AM Justice and Truth.

I Ask for your counselling to recall all of Who I AM, and to know my Divine Authority and Heritage. I AM Unconditional Love, for in embracing Justice and Truth, I See, Hear and Know through the Divine Truth of All-Knowing, the complete Journey of every Spiritual being. Therefore, I Judge not the Journey of another. For in truth we are All One and share the same Journey, the Journey of Spirit, and the Journey Home.

I AM in Gratitude and Give in Gracefully to the Universal Laws of Justice.

I Judge not; for in the eyes of God, I AM Love.
"And... So It Is

Invocation to the Sacred Violet Flame and Ray of Transmutation

I Call upon the Beloved Elohim: Arcturus and Victoria; Beloved Universal Logos: Lord Melchizedek; the Beloved Planetary Logos: Lord Gautama Buddha; The Planetary Hierarchy: Lord Sanat Kumara and Lady Venus; The Planetary Christ: Lord Maitreya; the Maha Chohan: Master St. Germain; and the Chohan: Lady Portia, and all the Masters and Lady Masters of the Violet Flame and Ray of Transmutation.

I Call upon Omri Tas from the Violet Planet, and Beloved Archangel Zadkiel and the Divine Complement Lady Amethyst, as witness to this invocation.

I Invoke the Sacred Violet Flame and Ray of Transmutation, Freedom and Forgiveness to permeate and saturate every Particle, Cell, Atom, Proton and Electron of my Spirit, Soul, and my four Body Systems, to replenish my entire being with the Violet Fire to my Divine Spiritual authority, Heritage and Truth.

I Request that I receive energy attunements to Higher Levels of Consciousness, and I Call upon Lady Portia to bring forth the Amplified Energetic frequencies that are designed to raise one's awareness to the Higher Dimensions of Consciousness.

I Ask Lady Portia for the Enlightenment that will allow me to be of greater assistance in bringing in the Cosmic Light Rays of Justice, Freedom of Opportunity, Forgiveness and Unconditional Love to Humanity. In turn this will Release the Veils of Forgetfulness from Humanity – revealing unto them the Truth of Who they really are as Children of God and to the Knowledge of their Divine Spiritual Heritage.

I Invoke in the name and authority of my Mighty I AM Presence into the World, the Divine Justice and Divine Truth of the Violet Fires of Freedom, Forgiveness, Unconditional Love, Compassion and Mercy. Planet Earth is Restored to the Divine Principles of the Violet Flame from the Violet Planet of Omri Tas.

Omri Tas, Lord of the Violet Planet from whence the Violet Flame originated and is generated, aides me and the Light Realms of Planet Earth, in the best way of using the Violet Flame and Ray of Transmutation, for the Highest Good of Planet Earth and the Highest Good of the Universe in accordance with the Divine Will of the Universal Logos: Lord Melchizedek.

My Feelings of Gratitude flood my world with waves upon waves of the Sacred Violet Flame and Ray of Transmutation, so that I AM quickly able to manifest the Divine Perfection of the New Golden Age in this now moment of time.

I AM Freedom, I AM Forgiveness and I AM Unconditional Love!
"And... So It Is!"

Prayer of the Violet Flame

I AM the Violet Flame, from the Violet Planet;

I AM the Violet Flame, and I invoke the Violet Fire;

I AM the Violet Flame, a Gift to Humanity from Lord Omri Tas;

I AM the Transmutation, of ALL to Love and Light;

I AM the Freedom, that Gives Opportunity for Growth;

I AM the Joy, that is Perpetiel Serenity;

I AM the Forgiveness, bringer of Peace to the Heart and Soul;

I AM the Transformation, that is Purification and Resurrection;

I AM the Diplomacy, the Art of Communication in Harmony;

I AM the Alchemy, the Science of Equilibrium and Immortality;

I AM the Balance of the Masculine and Feminine Principles;

I AM the Love and Serendipity of the Divine;

I AM the Justice, the Truth of All Knowing, that is Merciful;

I AM the Peace, the Christed Light Consciousness;

I AM the Violet Flame, the three-fold flame of your Heart and Soul;

I AM the Violet Flame, the Pathway to Oneness;

I AM the All that Is, the Violet Flame of God Consciousness;

Beloved Violet Flame of the Divine Principle I AM! "And... So It Is!"

(The Prayer of the Violet Flame came through to me from the Violet Flame itself. The Violet Flame is asking you, to be the energy of each one of these statements and to embrace the energy contained within. Speak this Prayer slowly and from the Living Energy of Your Heart Center). Hold in each of your hands an Amethyst Crystal, and the vibration of the Crystals will enhance your Prayer.

Prayer for the Temple of Grace

As I prepare myself for my Journey of Cosmic Ascension to even higher realms of Divine Consciousness, I Bring into my awareness the wondrous sound waves and frequencies of the Sacred Violet Flame and Ray of Transmutation, and the vibrations and frequencies of the Amethyst Crystals, which support and spiritually enhance the expansion of my Crown Chakra, thus creating a Divine "Temple of Grace."

I Invoke the Sounds of the Sacred Violet Flame and Ray, the Sound Masters of Transmutation and Transformation, to be a catalyst that expands and focuses my Soul Intention for Cosmic Ascension to the 5th Dimension and Beyond, with a clear connection to the Source of All That Is.

Within the Vibrations of the Sacred Violet Flame and Ray, I AM a Chalice of Light and Love. I Invoke Freedom and Unconditional Love into my lifestream, at all levels of my beingness.

As I Breathe in the Frequency created from the Sacred Flame and Ray of Transmutation, I AM in Balance and Harmony within my Sacred Heart, my Sacred Mind and my Sacred Soul.

I AM ONE with the Sacred Violet Flame and Ray. I Know Peace within My Soul.

Blessed I AM within the Temple of Grace.
"And... So It Is!"
(Imagine yourself in a circle of Violet Flame Fire and hold an Amethyst Crystal in each of your hands. Ask the Deva of the Amethyst Crystal to be with you and to bring you, your heartfelt desires).

Prayer for the Family Constellation

I AM That I AM and I Request of my Mighty I AM Presence and my Inner Divine, your assistance in the removal of all Aka cords that connect me with my family of origin in this life incarnation, and also to others from previous life incarnations.

I Request these Aka Cords to be severed with the Sword of Archangel Michael. I Request the connecting points to my Auric Sheathes, Etheric and Physical Body to be seared with the Sword of Archangel Michael to prevent further connections.

Archangel Michael check all my Auric Fields and Physical Body, to ensure that there are no Aka Cords connected to me whatsoever, as they are detrimental to my well-being and wellness.

I Release unto the Light Source within the Sacred Chambers of My Heart, all Family Constellation beliefs, patterns and programs that have controlled my Life, through the filters of my perceptions, both mentally and emotionally, of what I have made things mean about me during my Journey of shared experiences with family members.

I Declare myself to be in Acceptance of the Divine Perfection of all my family members.

I AM Grateful for all the experiences we have shared that have expanded my consciousness to higher levels of Awareness, Wisdom, Understanding and Love.

I Feel great Compassion for my family members in their journey and for the part we have all played in the evolutions of our Spirit and Souls, being both the teacher and the student in the experiences of life.

I Invoke the Sacred Violet Flame and Ray of Transmutation to surround each and every member of my Family Constellation, connecting us all together, with the energies of Freedom, Acceptance, Wisdom,

Understanding, Forgiveness and Unconditional Love, toward ourselves and each other.

I AM in Gratitude and Thank my Family of Origin in this Life Incarnation for all that we have experienced in our shared learnings in this lifetime together. We are Free to develop and grow through our shared experience within the Family.

Blessings of Freedom, Forgiveness and Unconditional Love to You All!
"And... So It Is!"

Prayer to Maha Chohan: Master St Germain – God of Freedom

Beloved Master St. Germain, God of Freedom that you are, I Call upon you to assist me in my Desire to have Greater Freedom in my life; Freedom from the mental and emotional pain that I experience in my physical body because of the unrest created by my thoughts and emotions, as they run rampart throughout my being.

I Ask for your Guidance in how best to deal with the issues and problems that emanate from my belief systems, which have been part of my Journey for so long, for many life times.

I Desire the Wisdom and Understanding from whence these issues and problems manifested, the knowledge of what meanings I gave to situations, which have been the cause of the mental and emotion turmoil that I AM experiencing in my Life until this current day – meanings that have ensnared and entrapped me even unto this now moment.

I Desire with all of my Heart to be Free – to feel the Freedom to be the Truth of my Spirit and the Truth of Who I AM as my True God-Self.

I Request access to the ceremony and application of the Science of True Alchemy, in order that I AM able to rise upon these situations, if this be for my Highest Good and the Highest Good of All.

I AM in Gratitude for all the help that you and the Sacred Violet Flame and Ray of Transmutation deliver to me.

I AM pledged to do whatever is needed of me in order to resolve the issues and problems that continue to keep me in the trauma and turmoil of my mind.

I AM That I AM. In Truth I AM the Light within
my Spirit and Soul and I AM Free.
"And... So It Is!"

Prayer to Lord Omri Tas of the Violet Planet

Lord Omri Tas of the Violet Planet, to you we of Humanity and Planet Earth are in deepest gratitude. For in your great Wisdom, Understanding, Compassion, Unconditional Love, Forgiveness and Freedom Energy, you saw a great need of the Sacred Violet Flame to be with us here on Planet Earth, to aid Planet Earth and All the Kingdoms and Realms of Earth.

I AM in Gratitude for your bestowing onto Humanity through the Maha Chohan, Master St. Germain, the Sacred Violet Flame and Ray of Transmutation. Thus Humanity has then been able to be embraced by the Violet Fire of the Flames of Transmutation to be in Forgiveness of Self and Others, Freedom and Unconditional Love.

Because of your Generosity of Spirit, and Your Great Love for The One, the Ultimate and Supreme God of All Creations, and in your Service to All That Is, we are able to raise our Consciousness to be in the Light and become Awakened, Enlightened and in Oneness with our God-Self and with others – and therefore in Oneness with All of Creation.

I AM Honored by the example that you have set before all to emulate as beings of Christed Light of God Consciousness.

I AM One with the Violet Flame of Transmutation.
I AM Free. "And... So It Is!"

Invocation to the Elohim: Arcturus and the Divine Complement Lady Victoria.

Beloved Elohim: Arcturus and Lady Victoria; the Universal Logos: Lord Melchizedek; Lord Omri Tas of the Violet Planet; the Maha Chohan: Master St. Germain and Lady Portia, Chohan of the Sacred Violet Flame and Ray of Transmutation; and my Beloved Mighty I AM Presence, Lord God essence of my being.

I Ask you to bring forth the Knowledge of the Divine Principles of Diplomacy and the Alchemy of the Sacred Flame and Ray of Transmutation, the Violet Flame that comes to aid Humanity and Planet Earth in this wondrous time of Planetary Ascension.

I Desire to attain greater Wisdom and Understanding of these Principles that I AM able, with this knowledge, to be of better service in the Transformation of myself, to higher levels of Christed Light of God Consciousness and to be the Unconditional Love of the Sacred Heart.

I AM That I AM in Service to The One, the All That Is.
"And... So It Is!"

Prayer to Archangel Zadkiel and the Divine Complement Lady Amethyst

Beloved Angels of Freedom and Unconditional Love, In the Light of Love I AM, I Call upon the Beloved Archangel of Freedom and Unconditional Love to be with me in this now moment.

Herald my return to Awareness, Peace and Acceptance for all my past and present misdemeanours.

I AM in the Embrace of Love Unconditional, for I Know that you, Archangel Zadkiel and the Divine Lady Amethyst, are here with me. Lost I have been in the shadows of my mind, returned I AM now; I AM to my Heart sublime. In the Christed Light of Love I AM.

Forever Freedom surrounds me as I Surrender to the All-Knowing of My Heart. In Gratitude and Grace, I AM before you, Beloved Angels of Freedom and Unconditional Love. I Thank You, Archangel Zadkiel and the Divine Complement Lady Amethyst, for your Guidance and the Unconditional Love that you bestow upon me.

From my Heart I emulate that Love to myself, others and all who are likewise in the heavenly fields of Mother/Father God, to be in One Unity Consciousness with myself, others and All the Kingdoms and Realms of Creation.

I AM Freedom and I AM Unconditional Love.
I AM Forever One with God! "And... So It Is!"

Sacred Flame of Transcendence – Image yourself within a Circle of Swirling Aqua and Sea Green Flame, at the core center of the Sacred Flame and Ray of Transcendence, Feel yourself taken beyond confusion to Certainty and Clarity.

Ray 8: The Aqua and Sea Green Ray

The Sacred Flame of Transcendence

Overlighted by: Helios & Vesta

Solar Council of Twelve

Chohan: Lady Nada

Archangel: Aquariel

Divine Complement: Lady Clarity

Key Attributes:

Certainty, Courage, Justice, Clarity, Integrity, Wisdom, Understanding,

Stability, Equilibrium, Unconditional Love,
Unity and Infinite Expansiveness;

Sacred Flame Energy Amplified on Wednesday

Transcendence beyond Confusion

to Certainty and Clarity

The Sea of Clarity!

Prayer to the Chohan: Lady Nada of the Sacred Flame and Ray of Transcendence

In the name and authority of my Beloved Mighty I AM Presence, Lord God essence of my being, I Call upon the Beloved Lady Nada, Chohan of the Sacred Flame and Ray of Transcendence, Beloved Lord Chietal, Archangel Aquariel and the Divine Complement Lady Clarity, All the Masters and Lady Masters of the Sacred Flame and Ray of Transcendence, and Beloved Lady Nada, blessings to you, beautiful Lady of Light.

I Ask that this Sacred Flame and Ray of Transcendence, Anchors and Activates my higher light energies, and Assists me in becoming the self-actualization of my truth as a Master of Light and Love and thereby create and manifest the qualities and sonic vibrations of certainty and clarity of purpose in my Life and on all levels of my being.

Blessings of the Sacred Flame and Ray of Transcendence – Certainty and Clarity – are with me and All of Humanity Now!

Thy Will Is Done, Thy Will is Done, Thy Will is Done.
Beloved I AM! "And... So It Is!"

Prayer for Certainty and Clarity

Beloved Lady Nada, I Come to you in this now moment that encompasses all time and space, in the Certainty of your Presence and Grace and I Receive in Gratitude from you the assured Blessings of Certainty and Clarity.

I See before me my Spiritual purpose, and through you, the feelings of Certainty in my Ascension into the Light of the 5th Dimension and beyond in this incarnation.

Blessings of Love to you Lady Nada, Chohan of the Aqua/Sea Green Ray: The Sacred Flame and Ray of Transcendence.

I Ask that waves upon waves of this wondrous energy flow over me, and immerse me into the higher vibration of Source Light that is this wonderful Ray's Influence.

In Certainty and Clarity I AM!
"And... So It Is!"

Prayer of Gratitude for the World

Beloved Chohan: Lady Nada. Masters and Lady Masters of the Sacred Flame and Ray of Transcendence, Archangel Aquariel and the Divine Complement Lady Clarity, and your Legions of Aqua/Sea Green Ray Angels.

I AM in Gratitude for your Presence and for your Blessings as they are made manifest into the world at this time.

I Ask that Planet Earth be surrounded and immersed into this amazing sonic vibration of transcendence, so that all beings of Planet Earth are awakened to the Certainty and Clarity of who they are and what they are as Spiritual beings of higher light vibrations and frequency from the Source of the All That Is.

I Invoke the Sacred Flame and Ray of Transcendence to be Anchored, Activated, Actualized and Amplified, for Humanity and All the Kingdoms and Realms of Planet Earth in this now moment of time.

I Ask that this be for the Highest Good of All
and the Highest Good for the Universe.
Thy Will Is Done, in and through me Now! "And... So It Is!"

Invocation to the Sacred Flame
and Ray of Transcendence

In the name and authority of my Mighty I AM Presence, I Invoke the Sacred Flame and Ray of Transcendence to encapsulate my entire being with the Sacred Fires of Aqua/Sea Green Light Energy, as I Embrace my Service role in Love, Integrity, Equilibrium and Balance.

I Trust and Surrender to my Mighty I AM Presence. I AM a Co-creator with the Company of Heaven and a Divine Keeper of the Cosmic Light, manifesting all that I Desire through my Service in Love and Light to the Glory of The One, the Ultimate and Supreme God of All Creations.

As I Embrace the Energy of Transcendence, I Expand and Deepen my Love of the Creator. I AM Living my Life in Truth, Harmony and Balance. I Let Go and Let God Heal all old memories, beliefs, patterns and programs that are irrelevant to my experience and ascension to the Light of Christ Consciousness, the Holy Spirit of my Being the True God-Self State that I AM.

I AM Embraced by the Energy of Transcendence,
I AM the Light of Christed Consciousness.
"And... So It Is!"

Prayer of Cleansing and Clearing

Blessed Sacred Flame and Ray of Transcendence, Sacred Flames of Aqua/Sea Green Fire, Bring your magnificent luminescent energy to assist in Cleansing and Clearing at a cellular level all my old false beliefs and judgements.

I AM Open to receive deep emotional healing from wounds that occurred to me in Ancient Days and Periods of the Earth's History. I have had incarnations in Lemuria, Atlantis, Egypt, Aztec, Inca, Mayan and Other Eras of time, which are still within my energetic fields to this current incarnation.

As Transmutation and Transformation are occurring, I Surround and Immerse myself within the Sacred Flame and Ray of Transcendence, it assists in recalibrating the Energy Bodies and bringing a renewed sense of balance and harmony to my entire Spiritual being, and to the building of my Lightbody which is related to the Sacred Geometry of the Merkebah.

In Grace and Gratitude I AM!

"And So It Is!"

Prayer to Balance and Harmonize My Mind

I Ask the Sacred Flame and Ray of Transcendence to help me to Balance my overly active Mind, bringing to me Clarity and Certainty and to also transmute all blockages from my being to Balance and Harmony.

I Embrace the Energetic properties of the wondrous Aqua/Sea Green Flame of the Sacred Flame and Ray of Transcendence in order to undergo a metamorphosis that will result in my receiving an entirely new, elevated Aqua/Sea Green Healing Vibration.

I AM Activated by the Sacred Flame and Ray of Transcendence. My Psychic Centers are Open and my Yang Energy is in alignment with my Yin Energy.

My Auric Fields are entrained for shifting, cleansing and activating my Upper Chakras. I Feel the Peace that comes from the Yang Energy and Color as they are activated to help Calm and bring Clarity to my analytical mind and lift my Spirits to Transcendence.

I Feel the Love that comes from my Yin Energy and Color as they are activated to help restore Equilibrium and Harmony to my thinking and emotional processes.

I AM Uplifted within my Mind and Heart by the Energy of this Sacred Flame and Ray to Oneness with my Heart, Mind and Soul.

Beloved Oneness I AM!
"And… So It Is!"

Invocation to the Elohim: Helios and Vesta and the Solar Council of Twelve

I Call upon the Mighty Helios and Vesta, Logos of the Solar System, and the Solar Council of Twelve, to bring to Humanity and All the Kingdoms and Realms of Planet Earth the Certainty and Clarity that are the Attributes of the Sacred Flame and Ray of Transcendence, to be with us in these turbulent times of Planet Earth's Solar Journey of Cosmic Ascension.

As the Destiny of Planet Earth expands and embraces the Cosmic Energies of the Solar System, these energies, vibrations and frequencies are to be transmuted, transformed and transfigured to transcend all to Balance and Harmony, and be for the Highest Good of Planet Earth, and All the Kingdoms and Realms of Earth.

The Elemental Kingdom in their role as Guardians brings in the upgraded energies that are to serve the Cosmic Ascension of Planet Earth with ease and grace.

I Desire from the Sacred Chambers of my Heart, that the Cosmic Ascension of Planet Earth be accomplished with the Certainty and Clarity of the Sacred Flame and Ray of Transcendence.

I Thank You, Beloved Helios and Vesta and the Solar Council of Twelve, I Honor You for Your Wisdom and Understanding.

I AM in Gratitude for All that you are.
"And… So It Is!"

Prayer to Archangel Aquariel and
Lady Clarity for Mother Earth

Beloved Archangel Aquariel, and the Divine Complement Lady Clarity, Divine Lady Nada, Lord Chietal and all the Masters and Lady Masters of the Sacred Flame and Ray of Transcendence.

I Ask you to encircle Mother Earth with the Sonic Vibrations of the Sacred Flame and Ray of Transcendence and Anchor, Activate, Actualize and Amplify these Energies into the Awareness of All Humanity, and thereby Awaken All to the Responsibility of being the Keepers of the Light and Love for this Sacred Planet, our Beloved Mother Earth.

Beloved Archangel Aquariel, Lady Clarity and the Pleiadian Emissaries of Light and Peace, Bless us all with the qualities of Courage, Justice, Integrity, Wisdom, Stability, Equilibrium, Unconditional Love, Understanding, Unity and Infinite Expansiveness, these are the attributes of the Sacred Fire of Transcendence, thus enabling us to be the Masters of the Sacred Flame and Ray of Transcendence, Clarity and Certainty for Mother Earth.

Thank You in Gratitude I AM!
"And... So It Is!"

Sacred Flame and Ray of Highest Potentials – Image yourself within a Circle of the Vibrant Magenta Flame, and at the central core of this beautiful Sacred Flame and Ray of Highest Potentials, You receive Divine Guidance in achieving your Highest Potentials.

Ray 9: Magenta Ray

The Sacred Flame of Highest Potentials

Synthesis of Rays 1 to 7

Overlighted by: Lord Goyana

Sirian Archangelic League of Light

Chohan: Lady Mother Mary

Archangel: Anthriel

Divine Complement: Lady Harmony

Key Attributes:

The Synthesis of Flames and Rays 1 to 7. Guidance in achieving one's Highest Potentials and in manifesting in life the Gifts that will assist in the Cosmic Ascension of One's Soul and Divine Guidance, Compassion, Unity, Justice, Peace, Order, Wisdom, Creativity, Mercy, Unconditional Love and Splendor.

Sacred Flame Energy Amplified on Tuesday

The Cradle of Love, Compassion

Divine Guidance to Highest Potentials!

Prayer to the Chohan: Lady Mother Mary.
Archangel Anthriel and Lady Harmony

Beloved Lady Mother Mary, Beloved Archangel Anthriel and the Divine Complement Lady Harmony of the Synthesis of Rays 1 to 7, and my Beloved Mighty I AM Presence, Lord God essence of my being.

I Invoke the Sacred Flame and Ray of Highest Potentials for the Synthesis of Rays 1 to 7 to Clear and Cleanse my Spirit, Soul, four Body Systems, Body Elemental, Inner Child and all Subtle Bodies.

I Ask that the elements and attributes that form this Synthesis transmute, transform and transfigure all negative aspects to the positive aspects of Surrender, Discipline, Illumination, Wisdom and Understanding, Unconditional Love, Compassion, Mercy, Purity, Perfect Health, Abundance, Resurrection and Restoration of the Divine Perfection of my Lightbody, Freedom and Forgiveness, to be the Divine Light and Divine Love That I AM.

I Invoke the Sacred Flame and Rays of Highest Potentials to manifest in my Life the Gifts that have been bestowed upon me by Mother/Father God through my Beloved Mighty I AM Presence, and for this to be done with ease and grace and for the Highest Good of All.

I AM committed to be of Service to Humanity and Mother Earth. And to fulfilling my Life Purpose in this incarnation by using the Gifts within me to achieve my Highest Potentials and to assist others to achieve their Highest Potentials and thereby bring Healing to Mother Earth.

Beloved Lady Mother Mary, Archangel Anthriel, and the Divine Complement Lady Harmony, I AM in Gratitude and I Thank You for Your Unconditional Love, Inner Peace and Harmony,

Blessings of Love, "And... So It Is!"

Prayer to be the Cradle of Love

Beloved Chohans of Unconditional Love, Lady Mother Mary, Lady Portia, Lady Nada, Lady Vessa Andromeda, Lady Quan Yin and Lady Pallas Athena. Beloved Sisterhood of Lemuria, Galatia, Angelina and Celeste,

I Open my Heart to Thee and ask that I AM taken within your most Holy Retreat of Love. I Desire with all my Heart to be embraced by your Love Essence – the Essence of the Divine Mother.

I AM Eternally Grateful for all the Love that I AM receiving from you. I Ask to BE the Love and Joy that you are. I Pledge, from my Heart to your Hearts, to BE Compassionate, Merciful, Unconditional Love, Harmonious and Peaceful. To BE as you and portray Love and Compassion to the world,

As I Walk through the World, wherever I dwell, I AM as You. As I AM as You, and All That Is, We are One Heart, the Cradle of Love.

The Cradle of Love I AM.
"And... So It Is!"

Prayer for My Highest Potentials

In the name of my Beloved Mighty I AM Presence, I Call upon Beloved Lady Mother Mary, Chohan of the Sacred Flame and Ray of Highest Potentials.

I Attract to me, my Fullest Potentials Now! I Call for a great Cosmic Beam of the Sacred Flame and Ray to attract to me my Crystalline Lightbody and Integrate my Crystalline Lightbody to all levels of my being Now!

I AM the Creative Extension of the Higher Mind of my Mighty I AM Presence. I Connect to the Realms of Illumined Truth in Wisdom, Joy, Splendor and Mercy.

I Experience my Highest Potentials through the merger and integration of my Higher God-Self of the Light and the Holy Christed I AM Presence of the Light.

I AM Love and Compassion in Physical Embodiment, I Manifest Creations of Light and Love, in accordance with the Divine Will of The One, the Ultimate, and Supreme God of All Creation.

Forever, I AM Love.
"And... So It Is!"

Prayer to Lord Goyana and the Sirian Archangelic League

I Call upon Lord Goyana, the Sirian Archangelic League of Light; Lady Mother Mary, Chohan of the Sacred Flame and Ray of Highest Potentials; and the Archangel Anthriel and the Divine Complement Lady Harmony, to assist Mother Earth and Humanity in achieving their Highest Potentials in this now moment of time.

I Invoke the Cosmic Flames and Rays of Light and the United, Integrated Twelve Sacred Flames and Rays to be of assistance to Mother Earth in her Ascension.

I Request that a great Cosmic Beam of the Sacred Flame and Rays of Highest Potentials attracts to Mother Earth her Crystalline Lightbody and to Anchor, Activate, Actualize and Amplify her Crystalline Lightbody to All levels of her being Now!.

I Ask that this be for the Highest Good of Mother Earth and the Highest Good of All.

I Thank You, Beloved Lady Mother Mary, Beloved Lord Goyana and the Sirian Archangel League of Light and the Archangel Anthriel and Lady Harmony, for helping us all to achieve our Highest Potentials.

So be it now. "And... So It Is!"

Prayer of Gratitude to Lady Mother Mary

Beloved Lady Mother Mary, Queen of Hearts, I AM in Deepest Gratitude for your Unfailing Unconditional Love and Compassion that you have in your Divine Spiritual Perfection of the Christed Light Consciousness showered upon the Children that are Humanity.

I Love you, Beloved Mother Mary, from the Sacred Chambers of My Heart to your Sacred Heart. I Send the Blessings of my Eternal Love for you and my Heartfelt Gratitude for your Life.

Thank You, Beloved Mother of Love.
Beloved I AM! "And... So It Is!"

Prayer of the Rose

Beloved Lady Mother Mary, you are the Rose, the Beautiful Flower in the Crown of Heaven that adorns my Heart. Through your example, I AM shown the way of Love, Compassion, Peace, Mercy and Forgiveness.

I Desire from my entire being to BE as you are and to speak as you speak. In achieving this, my voice holds the vibration and frequency of your voice – the Love Resonance of your Heart.

You are the Rose that Adorns my Heart. As you are I AM, I too become the Rose – the Beautiful Flower in the Crown of Heaven.

Beloved Mother/Father God and my Beloved Mighty I AM Presence, I Pledge to be in Service to Humanity, and to aid our dearly Beloved Lady Mother Mary, Lord Goyana, the Archangel Anthriel and the Divine Complement Lady Harmony, and the Sirian League of Light to Assist Humanity in connecting to their Hearts, and fulfilling the Divine Plan of their Highest Potentials, and the Restoration of their Light Body of Perfection.

I AM the Rose.
"And... So It Is!"

> Sacred Flame and Ray of Divinity – Image yourself within a
> Circle of Pearlescent Fire. Feel yourself at the core center of the
> Sacred Pearlescent Flame and Ray – surrounded and embraced
> by the Shimmering energy of Inner Divinity and Peace.

Ray 10: The Pearlescent Ray.

The Sacred Flame and Ray of Divinity

Overlighted by: Lord Huertal

Andromedan Intergalactic Beings of Light

Chohan: Lady Vessa Andromeda

Archangel: Valoel

Divine Complement: Lady Peace

Key Attributes:

Peace, Balance, Equilibrium, Justice, Power, Infinite Wisdom,

Detachment, Attainment, Responsibility, Self-Mastery,
Opulence, Divinity and Transcendence to the God-
Self State of The One, the Supreme Creator God.

Sacred Flame Energy Amplified on Friday

The Shimmering Sacred Pearlescent Flame of Peace

Divine Inner Peace!

Prayer to the Chohan: Lady Vessa Andromeda. Archangel Valoel and Lady Peace

Beloved Chohan: Lady Vessa Andromeda. Beloved Archangel Valoel and the Divine Complement Lady Peace, Master Allah Gobi and the Andromeda Council of Elders, the Intergalactic Emissaries of Light.

I Know the Truth of my Spiritual Divinity that I AM as you are. As I Feel the Christed Light of God Consciousness Energy within me, I AM Living in the Light of my Divinity and in Divine Opulence.

I AM shown the way to recognize the Spiritual Divinity that I AM. And to see, feel and hear the Divine Energy of the Christed Light of God Consciousness as it releases from my being, all that is not of the Divine Light and Inner Peace; and that this be for my Highest Good and the Highest Good of All.

I Embrace the Sacred Flame and Ray of Divinity. I AM in Gratitude to this vibrant Pearlescent Flame and Ray, as it blazes forth sending its powerful Rays of Divinity to Encapsulate my entire being and lift my consciousness to be in Balance, Inner Peace and Harmony. And to be the Wisdom and Understanding of the All-Knowing of my Mighty I AM Presence.

Divine Inner Peace I AM!
"And... So It Is!"

Prayer to the Pearlescent Fire

I Embrace the Pearlescent Fire, as its Shimmering Pearlescent Light transforms the negativity that is present here on Mother Earth, into the Divinity of the Christed Light of God Consciousness.

The Sacred Flames and Rays of Pearlescent Fire in their Opulence are raised high into the atmosphere, and Surround All Humanity and Mother Earth with waves upon waves of Sacred Pearlescent Flames and Rays of Divinity, Opulence and Inner Peace. The Divine Light of Inner Peace and the Sacred Flames and Rays of Divinity enter into All the Kingdoms and Realms of Mother Earth.

Oh Gracious Lady Vessa Andromeda, Chohan of the Sacred Shimmering Pearlescent Fire that is the Sacred Flame and Ray of Divinity, I AM Grateful for your Presence, in your being here for Mother Earth.

I Give Thanks to Master Allah Gobi and the Andromeda Council; Intergalactic Emissaries of the Light, for their aid in awakening Humanity to the Truth of their Divinity in this now moment of all Time and Space.

In Gratitude, I Thank You All. Awakened to My Divinity I AM!
"And... So It Is!"

Prayer to Anchor the Crystalline Lightbody

My Beloved Mighty I AM Presence, Lord God essence of my being. The Chohan: Lady Vessa Andromeda, of the Sacred Flame and Ray of Divinity.

I AM the Divine embodiment of the Sacred Flame and Ray of Divinity.

I AM the Divine Expression of Inner Peace and Opulence.

I AM Power, Love, and Light, in Balance and Harmony.

I AM Infinite Wisdom and Detachment as I Experience the Higher Mind of The One, the Ultimate and Supreme God of All Creations, through the integration of my Mighty I AM Presence, my Higher Light. All levels of forgetfulness are lifted; I now experience the Immortal Aspect of my True Nature. I AM in my Self-Mastery and Spiritual Divinity Now!

The Power and Divinity of the Sacred Flame and Ray have changed my four Body Systems to be Crystalline. I AM merged with my Spirit and Soul.

The programs of Spiritual Divinity, Inner Peace and Opulence have been encoded into my Mental, Emotional, Physical Body and Body Elemental.

I Anchor my Crystalline Lightbody fully into my being. I integrate my Crystalline Lightbody at all levels, as this is integral to my achieving my Cosmic Ascension in this lifetime.

I Call upon Lady Vessa Andromeda, Lord Huertal and the Andromeda Intergalactic Emissaries of Light, to assist me in the attainment of my Spiritual Divinity, Opulence and Inner Peace, and in the Mastery of the Cosmic Christed Light of God Consciousness Energy that is my God-Self State — by the full Activation and Amplification of my Crystalline Lightbody in this Life incarnation.

I AM That I AM, I AM my Crystalline Lightbody. "And... So It Is!"

Prayer to Crystalline my Physical Body

My Beloved Monad, my Mighty I AM Presence and my Higher Self, I Ask of you and my guides to assist me in every way possible to bring my Physical Body into crystallization, the Crystalline Lightbody of my fulfilled, Perfectly Healthy Physical Body of Light.

My Physical Body and my Body Elemental are to be crystalline and in alignment with my Etheric and Spiritual Beingness, my Soul.

I Command that all the negative energies contained within my four Body Systems be transformed, transmuted and transfigured by the United Sacred Flames and Rays of Christed Light of God Consciousness to be in alignment with my Physical Body as being of the Crystalline Lightbody Energy.

I Release All Belief Systems from my Spirit, Soul, Mind and Body that are core causal, and effect memory records, that are detrimental to my Physical Body and Body Elementals crystallization. All Mental and Emotional Beliefs, Patterns and Programs, on all levels of my Physical Body and Energetic Systems, are restored, rejuvenation and resurrected to the New Encodement of Divine Perfection of my Crystalline Lightbody.

All aspects of my physical being at the Cellular, Atom, Electron, Proton and Neutron levels are encapsulated by the Holy Spirit and the Christed Light of God Consciousness of The One, the Ultimate and Supreme God of All Creations.

My Physical Being is restored to the Perfection of Health that creates the Divine Crystalline Physical Lightbody. My Heart is in control of manifesting my Crystalline Lightbody, and my entire being Spiritual, Soul, Mental, Emotional and my Physical body – recognize my Heart as being in Charge of My Life.

I AM Living from My Heart in All Situations. "For this I Give Thanks, And... So It Is!"

Prayer for Building My Crystalline Lightbody

My Beloved Mighty I AM Presence, Lord God essence of my being. I Call upon the Beloved Cosmic Logos: Avatar of Synthesis: the Mahatma. The Beloved Universal Logos: Lord Melchizedek. The Beloved Maha Chohan and Chohans of the Twelve Sacred Flames and Rays of Christed Light of God Consciousness; to be present in this now moment of time.

I Call upon the Energy of the Cosmic Logos: Avatar of Synthesis: the Mahatma to assist me in Building the Antakarana, all the way to the Source of All That Is, to the Christed Light of God Consciousness of The One, the Ultimate and Supreme God of All Creations.

The Energy of the Cosmic Logos: Avatar of Synthesis: the Mahatma is within me and accelerates my Ascension Processes, clearing the Veils of Forgetfulness, to be Unconditional Self-Love, Wisdom and Understanding, achieving the 5th Dimensional Levels of Higher Consciousness and Beyond to the Multi-Dimensions of Christed Light of God Consciousness and the Building of my Crystalline Lightbody.

I Affirm that this is done with ease and grace and in accordance with my Divine Purpose for this incarnation. And that everything is for my Highest Good and the Highest Good of All.

I AM Connected to the Source of All That Is. "And So It Is!"

Prayer to the Divine Cosmic Mother

Beloved Divine Cosmic Mother, as you give birth to the sounds of the Divine Mother/Gaia/Virgo, I AM Carried forth by your resonances and peace to the comfort of the energy of Venus, the Goddess of Love. I Feel your Divine Cosmic Love.

I Surrender to the Nurturing vibrations of the water elementals, and I Feel the ever-present and fullness of the Spirit of Your Divinity.

I AM Complete, I AM Embraced by the sounds and tones of your essence. I AM Free and Tranquil. I AM at Peace within myself. And as my emotional issues drift away from my awareness, I Discover within myself my Divinity and Oneness with my Mighty I AM Presence, my True God-Self.

Beloved Divine Cosmic Mother of Harmony, as you lift up my Life Force Energy, I AM Borne on the Crest of your Sound Waves to Higher Levels of Consciousness. I AM Grateful and I Honor your Sounds of Cosmic Love and Compassion.

Blessed I AM. "And... So It Is!"

Prayer for Peace on Planet Earth

My Mighty Monad and my I AM Presence, Lord God essence of my being be with me now, as I Call upon the Beloved One, the Ultimate and Supreme God of All Creation, the Beloved Universal Logos: Lord Melchizedek. The Beloved Planetary Logos: Lord Gautama Buddha. And the Beloved Planetary Christ: Lord Maitreya to be present in this now moment of time.

I Reach out with all of my Sacred Heart, Spirit, Soul, Mind and Might for Peace on Earth and Good Will toward all Humanity, All the Kingdoms and Realms of Planet Earth, from the Cosmic Heart, Mind and Will of God.

I Call forth the Full Divine Intervention of the Godforce to bring Peace and Harmony through the Energy of the Christed Light of God Consciousness, and Cosmic Love, Wisdom and Understanding of The One, the All That Is, to All the troubled Regions of Planet Earth.

I Desire with all my Sacred Heart, Spirit, Soul, Mind and Might that God's Divine Plan of Peace and Harmony for Planet Earth is manifested in this now moment of time.

God's Divine Plan is Anchored, Activated, and Amplified into all Regions of Planet Earth Now!

I Thank you and Accept this as being done in Accordance with God's Will, the Divine Will in the Divine Perfection of All That Is.

"And... So It Is!"

Invocation to Lord Huertal and the Andromedan Intergalactic Beings of Light

Beloved Lord Huertal and the Andromedan Intergalactic Beings of Light; Beloved Lady Vessa Andromeda, Chohan of the Sacred Flame of Divinity, and the Beloved Archangel Valoel and the Divine Complement Lady Peace.

As I Embrace my Divinity, I Invoke the Sacred Flame and Ray of Divinity, Peace and Opulence to permeate my entire being – my Spirit and Soul, my Chakra System, every Particle, Cell, Atom, Proton, Electron and Neutron, with waves upon waves of powerful Pearlescent Fire, the Shimmering Flame of Peace, surging through me and bringing to me Inner Peace and Opulence.

I Command that the Sacred Flame and Ray of Divinity encapsulates every particle of my Etheric and Auric Fields, my Spirit and Soul, passing upwards through the higher levels of my Chakra System to the Universal, Solar and Multidimensional levels of my Christed Divine God-Self State, bringing me back to the Oneness of my Holy God-Self.

I AM in Deepest Gratitude to Lord Huertal and the Andromedan Intergalactic Beings of Light, and Lady Vessa Andromeda, for being the embodiment of the Sacred Flame and Ray of Divinity.

I Reclaim my Divinity and I Live in Inner Peace and Opulence Now!

I AM my Divine God-Self State.
"And... So It Is!"

Sacred Flame and Ray of Illumined Truth – Image yourself within a Circle of Peach Flame and at the core center of the Sacred Flame and Ray of Divine Illuminated Truth, View before you the Truth of Who you are and See the Truth of what you are here in this incarnation to learn.

Ray 11: The Peach Ray.

The Sacred Flame of Illumined Truth

Overlighted by: Lord Semveta

Brotherhood of Light

Chohan: Lady Quan Yin

Archangel: Perpetiel

Divine Complement: Lady Joy

Key Attributes:

Illumine Truth, Joy, Serenity, and Activation, Awakened and Awareness of Their Truth, Compassion and Mercy, Rebirth and Rejuvenation, Understanding, Strength, Stability, Loving Kindness, Wisdom, Generosity, Abundance, Compassion, Balance, Organization and Discernment.

Sacred Flame Energy Amplified on Thursday

Seeker of the Illumine Truth of my Life

Divine Truth Illuminated!

Prayer to the Chohan: Lady Quan Yin for Illumined Truth

Beloved Lady Quan Yin, Chohan of the Sacred Flame and Ray of Illumine Truth, Beloved Lord Semveta and the Brotherhood of Light.

I AM a Seeker of the Illumine Truth of my Life. I Ask for the Wisdom and Understanding of the Sacred Flame and Ray, as I become more awakened and aware of the truth of Who I AM and what my purpose is for being in this incarnation.

I Pray to you, Beloved Lady Quan Yin for Humanity, that all who are Seekers of the Truth of who they are, be granted their desires and become Activated, Awakened and Aware of the Oneness of all things. And that they learn to dwell within the Heart Flame of their Heart and know the Love and Light of their Divine I AM Presence, the God-Self within.

I AM my Divine I AM Presence.

"And... So It Is!"

Prayer for Joy and Serenity

Beloved Archangel Perpetiel and the Divine Complement Lady Joy, I AM in Deepest Gratitude for the Boundless Joy that is in my Life.

I Feel the Serenity and the Peace which that brings, filling up my entire being with the Love of Archangel Perpetiel and Lady Joy. I AM in the Balance and Harmony that is Joy and Serenity.

I Know that you are with me in all areas of my Life, helping me to see, feel and hear the Joyfulness that emanates from my family, my friends and from my fellow Humanity.

I See the Hidden Joyfulness within me now. I AM that JOY, I AM that JOY in all things, and thereby know and feel the Deepest Serenity within my Spirit and Soul.

In Gratitude I AM for your Service to ALL.
Thank you, Beloved Archangel Perpetiel and Lady Joy.
"And... So It Is!"

Prayer for Past Life Recall

In my Life, I Dream of the Lives that I have been.
I remember the Life experiences; I recreate the experiences in my Life.
In my Life, I Re-create the lives that I have been.
I Know not in consciousness and therefore,
I Desire to Recall the Lives that I have lived.

In my Life, I Desire to be Free of the Lives that I have been.
In Illumine Truth, I recall the Lives that I have lived and seen,
So that I AM Healed of all the negativity that these lives bring
and affect me NOW in this Life I AM in.

In my Life, I AM Free of the Lives that I have been.
I AM Wise and Understanding because of the Lives that I have lived,
I AM Living my Life in Truth and I AM Free.
I AM In Oneness with the Lives that I have been.
I AM Truly Blessed by the Truth of My Past Life Recall.
And So It Is but One Life in All – It is what it is, Divine Perfection.
"And... So It Is!"

Invocation to the Sacred Flame and Ray of Illumined Truth

I AM that I AM and in the name and authority of my Mighty I AM Presence. I Invoke the Sacred Flame and Ray of Illumine Truth, Joy and Serenity, to come forth and illuminate to my Conscious Mind, the Truth of my Life.

I AM Aware in Consciousness of all that which I AM, all that which I AM Destined to become, in the restoration of the Divinity of my Highest Potentials, with Certainty, Clarity and One Unity Consciousness of my True God-Self State.

I AM the Representation of the Illumine Truth of my Life. I Live in Awakened Awareness of all that I AM. I AM Totally Dedicated to Living my Life in the Joy and Serenity of Illumine Truth.

I AM Grateful to the Chohan: Lady Quan Yin, for the Compassion and Mercy that she embodies. I AM thankful to the Archangel Perpetiel and the Divine Complement Lady Joy, for the Presence that they bring into my Life, the energy frequency and vibration of Perpetiel Joy and Love that is the Illumine Truth.

It is What It Is and I AM in Divine Acceptance of the Divine
Perfection of What It Is. All That Is, Blessed I AM.
"And... So It Is!"

Prayer to Awaken Humanity to the Illumine Truth of Planet Earth

Beloved Lord Semveta and the Great White Brotherhood of Light; As Humanity and All the Kingdoms and Realms of Planet Earth, sit upon the brink of great changes coming from the Universal Logos: Lord Melchizedek. The Solar System of Helios and Vesta and the Galactic Logos: Lord Melchior, Let there be Peace, Harmony and Balance in their Awakening.

I Call upon Lord Semveta and the Great White Brotherhood of Light to Awaken Humanity to the Illumine Truth of the Mother, Virgo/Gaia the sentient being that inhabits Planet Earth, and who they are as custodians and guardians of her Wellbeing and Perfect Health.

The Cosmic Rays, Anchor, Activate, Actualize and Amplify the energies of Illumine Truth into Humanity, to Awaken Humanity to the Illumine Truth of the Planet, and expand this Awareness throughout the many levels of Consciousness that are present here on Earth and in All the Kingdoms and Realms of Planet Earth.

Humanity Awakens to the Truth of who they are and what they need to do, in order to be in the Flow of Life and in Oneness within themselves and with each other and All the Kingdoms and Realms of this great Planet, which is Home to Mother, Virgo/Gaia, many different beings, and of many different species and life streams.

The Sacred Flame and Ray of Illumine Truth send waves upon waves of the Sacred Fire, to Planet Earth, surrounding Planet Earth, and All that dwell therein – with the Joy and Serenity that comes with the Awakening to the Truth of the Oneness of All Things.

Illumine Truth brings Joy and Serenity!
"And... So It Is!"

Prayer to Archangel Perpetiel and the Divine Complement Lady Joy

My Beloved I AM Presence, Lord God essence of my being, as I Call upon the Beloved Archangel Perpetiel and the Divine Complement Lady Joy, and the Beloved Lady Quan Yin, I Embrace the Joy and Serenity of this Sacred Flame and Ray of Illumine Truth to my Heart, Mind, Body and Soul.

I Honor you with the Truth of my Heart, I AM surrounded in the Sacred Flame and Ray of Illumine Truth, which allows me to express my Spiritual Reality in increased discernment and Abundance in Health.

The Sacred Flame and Ray of Illumine Truth heals my lower bodies and Rejuvenates and Regenerates my organs and physical body to the New Encodements of Divine Perfection.

The Sounds that Emanate from my Organs, my Physical Body and my Skin are the Sounds of Health and Vitality. I AM in Wellness of Mind, Body, Spirit and Soul.

I experience Rebirth and Rejuvenation through the Cosmic Heart, Mind and Will of God. I AM Reborn into the Divinity of the Creator, the All That Is.

I AM thankful to Archangel Perpetiel and the Divine Complement Lady Joy for bringing Serenity and Joy into my Life.

I AM Eternally Grateful, Beloved Lady Quan Yin. I Honor You for your Compassion and Mercy. I AM in Gratitude to my Mighty I AM Presence for I AM Joyous and in Serenity.

Merciful and Compassionate I AM!
"And... So It Is!"

Prayer to the Angels of Illumine Truth

Beloved Archangel Perpetiel, the Divine Complement Lady Joy and All the Angels of Illumine Truth; I AM with you now. I Feel your Presence Surrounding my Auric Fields as you aid me in the Removal of my Masks, the Masks that had block me from being the Truth of Who I AM.

I AM in my Truth and I AM Transparent in speaking my Truth. I AM Living the Life that I was Born to Live.

Archangel Perpetiel, Lady Joy and All the Angels of Illumine Truth, fill me with the energy of Courage and Compassion.

I AM in Truth and therefore I AM able to face the Truth about myself. I See the Truth of my Life and in Acceptance I Know that I AM Enlightened.

I AM Serenity and Joy, because I See through the Masks of Illusion and realize the Truth of who I AM. I AM my Divine God-Self.

I AM the Mind of God having the experience of the Illusions, the experience of the Lies. I AM my True God-Self and I AM Grateful to Archangel Perpetiel, Lady Joy and All the Angels of Illumine Truth – for their expression of the Truth.

I Acknowledge the Great Good that you are doing for Planet Earth and the Universe.

Thank You for the Illumine Truth that you are, which is aiding me to be the Truth of who I AM. "And... So It Is!"

> Sacred Flame and Ray of One Unity Consciousness – Image yourself within a Circle of Golden Fire, and at the core center of the Sacred Golden Opalescent Flames and Rays of One Unity Consciousness with Self and Others, Feel in Oneness with All things and the Oneness you have with The One, the Supreme Creator God of All That Is.

Ray 12: The Golden Opalescent Ray.

The Sacred Flame of One Unity Consciousness

Overlighted by: Lord Ardal

Cosmic Logos: The Avatar of Synthesis: the Mahatma and Lord Melchizedek

Chohan: Lady Pallas Athena

Archangel: Omniel

Divine Complement: Lady Opalescence

Key Attributes:

Acceptance of what is – as Divine Perfection, Oneness with All Things, Transfiguration, Balance and Harmony, Connection to All That Is, Inner Peace and Tranquillity.

Divine Qualities: Wisdom, Devotion, Illuminating Intelligence, Love, Power, Harmony, Peace, Equilibrium, Creativity, Inspiration, Magnetism, Enlightenment and One Unity Consciousness.

Sacred Flame Energy Amplified on Sunday

One Unity Consciousness with Self

Transfiguration to Divine Oneness!

Prayer to the Chohan: Lady Pallas Athena, Archangel Omniel and Lady Opalescence

Beloved One, the Ultimate and Supreme God of All Creations, the All That Is, the Beloved Chohan: Lady Pallas Athena, the Archangel Omniel and the Divine Complement, Lady Opalescence, Lord Ardal and the Cosmic Logos: the Avatar of Synthesis: the Mahatma; and the Universal Logos: Lord Melchizedek.

I Call upon Lady Pallas Athena, the Masters and Lady Masters of the Sacred Flame and Ray of One Unity Consciousness and the Archangel: Omniel and Lady Opalescence.to assist me, as I Call forth the Twelfth Sacred Flame and Ray of One Unity Consciousness.

I Invoke the Sacred Flame and Ray of One Unity Consciousness in order to create the New Golden Age of Oneness, Peace and Harmony. I AM a Christed Light Conscious Being in service to All Life, to Humanity and All the Kingdoms and Realms of Planet Earth.

I AM Free of the veils of forgetfulness, revealed unto me are the gifts that have been bestowed upon me by the Holy Spirit of All That Is, which will enable me to be of greater service to Humanity, and for All the Kingdoms and Realms Planet Earth.

I Now access the Hidden Knowledge that is held within my being, which will enable me to fulfil my Life Purpose, and be of One Unity Consciousness. I Experience the Sacred Flame and Ray of One Unity Consciousness, within my Immortal Nature and the Cosmic Embrace of The One, the All That Is. .

I AM Connected and in Total Oneness and Complete Remembrance, with the Source of All Life, the All That Is. I AM incorporated within the Divine Mission of the Planetary Hierarchy to actively create and manifest the New Golden Age of One Unity Consciousness, through the Unconditional Love and Christed Light of The One, the Ultimate and Supreme God of All Creations, the All That Is! "And... So It Is!"

Prayer of Surrender to Oneness

Beloved One, the Ultimate and Supreme God of All Creations, the Beloved Lady Pallas Athena, my Mighty I AM Presence, Lord God essence of my being, my Higher Self, Beloved Mother Earth, Lady Gaia/Virgo.

Planetary Hierarchy: Lord Sanat Kumara and Lady Venus. Planetary Christ: Lord Maitreya. Planetary Logos: Lord Gautama Buddha. Maha Chohan: Master St. Germain. Beloved Chohan: Lady Pallas Athena of the Sacred Flame and Ray of One Unity Consciousness.

Ascended Masters and Lady Masters of the Sacred Flame and Ray of One Unity Consciousness, Beloved Archangel: Omniel and the Divine Complement Lady Opalescence; and the Golden Angels of One Unity Consciousness.

I Surrender in Oneness to the Heart of God. I AM the
Heart of God. I Love all beings of the Cosmic All, as from
the Heart Consciousness of God, Love Unconditional.
I Surrender in Oneness to the Mind of God. I AM the
Mind of God. As God is, so I AM, God's thoughts are
my thoughts. I AM Balanced and in Harmony.
I Surrender in Oneness to the Will of God. I AM the Will
of God. Therefore, I Follow the Plan of God and Obey
God's Universal Laws of Oneness with All things.
I AM One with God, I AM All That Is.
I Surrender in Oneness to The One, the Ultimate and
Supreme God of All Creations, All the negative energies held
within my Soul, my four Body systems, All Subtle Bodies,
Body Elemental and Inner Child. I Receive the Wisdom and
Understanding of these negative energies with ease and grace.

I Surrender in Oneness to The One, the Ultimate and Supreme
God of All Creations, All the Patterns and Programs held
within my being that have still to be Resolved, Balanced and
Harmonized, in order for my Cosmic Ascension to ever Higher
Levels of Consciousness to occur. I Receive the Wisdom and
Understanding of these Patterns and Programs with ease and grace.
I Surrender in Oneness to The One, the Ultimate and Supreme God
of all Creations, All the Pain and Grief that I have held within me,
that I have endured since the beginning of my Spiritual Journey.

I Request that you hear my words as I Pledge to you my Service to
the Heart, Mind and Will of God. I Affirm that all is for the Highest
Good and in Accordance with the Divine Will of The One, the Ultimate,
Supreme God of All Creation.

Surrendered to the Oneness that I AM!
"And... So It Is!"

Prayer: I Surrender to the Heart of God

I Surrender to the Heart of God – I AM the Heart of God, I Love all beings of the Cosmic All as from the Heart Consciousness of God, Love Unconditional. I AM One with God. I AM All That Is.

I Surrender to the Heart of God – All the negative energies held within my four Body Systems, All Subtle Bodies, Body Elemental and Inner Child, I Receive the Wisdom and Understanding of these negative energies with ease and grace.

I Surrender to the Heart of God – All Old Beliefs, Patterns and Programs held within my being, that have still to be Resolved, Balanced and Harmonized; in order for my Cosmic Ascension to the 5th Dimension and Beyond to occur. I Receive the Wisdom and Understanding of these Old Beliefs, Patterns and Programs with ease and grace.

I Surrender to the Heart of God – All my Pain and Grief from my beingness – that has been with me since the beginning of my Spiritual Journey.

From the Sacred Chambers of my Heart, I Pledge my Service to the Heart, Mind and Will of God. I Affirm that all is and has been for the Highest Good of All and in accordance with the Divine Will of The One, the Ultimate and Supreme God of All Creations.

Beloved I AM! "And… So It Is!"

Prayer for I AM One Unity Consciousness

Beloved Chohan: Lady Pallas Athena of the Sacred Flame and Ray of One Unity Consciousness. Archangel: Omniel and the Divine Complement Lady Opalescence, and the Golden Angels of One Unity Consciousness. Beloved Universal Logos: Lord Melchizedek.

I AM One Unity Consciousness. I AM as you are, and as I AM One Unity Consciousness All Limitations fall away. I AM held within the essence of the Creator that is only Cosmic Love and Enlightenment. I AM Limitless and I AM Strong. I Feel the Strength within me that encourages me to go forth and allows me to be a pure vessel for the Sacred Light that is the Cosmic Light and Cosmic Love of The One, the Ultimate and Supreme God of All Creations, the All That Is.

I AM Accepting the Light and Love Information from the All That Is, with every Breath That I AM. As I fulfil my Cosmic Ascension pathway, I Feel the Limiting Beliefs falling away from me. I AM holding this Light Energy of Love and All-Knowing. I AM creating within me the Sacred Humble Loving Strength that comes from the Wisdom and Understanding of my Beloved Mighty I AM Presence. I AM Pure of Heart. I AM Clear in Mind.

I AM Devoted to Being of Service to The One, the Ultimate, Supreme God of All Creation, the All That Is, and to the Return of the Remembrance of Who I AM in Truth, therefore, I AM Free from the attachments to the physical realms of Planet Earth.

I AM Totally Healed. My Divine Connection to the Holy Spirit of The One, is Enhanced, and in so being Enables me to Create the Healing for Humanity, All the Kingdoms and Realms of Earth, Planet Earth and the Universe.

I AM One Unity Consciousness.
"I AM All That Is, And... So It Is!"

Prayer for Creating Abundance with One Unity Consciousness

Beloved Lady Pallas Athena, Chohan of the Sacred Flames and Ray of One Unity Consciousness; Beloved Cosmic Logos: Avatar of Synthesis: the Mahatma; and the Beloved Maha Chohan and the Chohans of the Twelve Sacred Flames and Rays of Christed Light of God Consciousness.

I Call upon the Sacred Flame and Ray of One Unity Consciousness and the Integrated and United Twelve Sacred Flames and Rays of Light to pour over and throughout my entire being the Powerful Vibrations and Qualities of The One, the Ultimate and Supreme God of All Creations, that you hold. Remove or bring to the surface of my mind for Release, the Vibrations and Awareness of Lack, especially that which is connected to the Lack of the Creator being in my Life.

I Release from my Belief System all energies that are of Lack, to the Sacred Flame and Ray of One Unity Consciousness and to the Integrated, United Twelve Sacred Flames and Rays of Christed Light of God Consciousness, to be Transfigured, Transmuted and Transformed to the Abundance of One Unity Consciousness.

I AM Now Free of the Consciousness Energy around Lack of any kind. I Realize that Abundance has always been a Powerful Energy within me, which I AM Eternally using to fuel my creations, with the Power of the Sacred Golden Flame and Ray of Oneness and the United Multi-colored Sacred Flames and Rays of Christed Light of God Consciousness. I AM Experiencing the Abundance of the Creator of All That Is.

I Boost the Abundance of the Creator That I AM. I AM Anchoring the Abundance of the Creator to me Now! I AM assisting myself in Energetically Experiencing Abundance in Wealth, Health and Relationships with myself, Others and the Universe. Love and Light pulsate throughout my being now and eternally.

I AM Connected to the Abundance Vibration of the Creator. I AM in my Divinity. I AM Experiencing Resonance with the Abundance Vibration of the Creator. Abundance is a Natural Aspect of my being that has always resided within my Energy Essence.

I Claim My Right to this Abundance Now!
Abundant I AM! "And… So It Is!"

Invocation to Lord Ardal and the Cosmic Logo: the Avatar of Synthesis: the Mahatma.

In the name and authority of my Beloved Mighty I AM Presence, Lord God Essence of my Spirit, I Reach Out to you Lord Ardal and to the Cosmic Logos: Avatar of Synthesis, the Mahatma; to Anchor and Activate within me the Consciousness that is of the Mahatma energy for One Unity Consciousness.

I Invoke the Presence of Lord Ardal and the Mahatma Energy to dissolve the crystallized and fixed meanings, beliefs, patterns and programs that are locked into my Spirit, Soul, my four Body Systems, my Inner Child and Body Elemental.

I Call forth the frequency and vibration energy of Lord Ardal and the Mahatma Energy, so that the higher frequency and vibration of their energy will enable and facilitate my attaining the Higher Levels of Consciousness that are necessary for my Cosmic Ascension to my Spiritual God-Self State of the Holy Spirit of One Unity Consciousness.

The Over-lighting Energy of Lord Ardal and the Mahatma Energy blazes forth throughout all levels of my being, bringing me to the ultimate goal of raising my Spirit, Soul, all my four Body Systems, Auric Fields, Universal, Solar and Multidimensional Systems into the frequency of light and into the integrated energies of the Sacred Flame and Ray of One Unity Consciousness and, therefore, into the energy of the Cosmic Rays of Service.

I AM in Gratitude to Lord Ardal for Over-lighting the Sacred Flame and Ray of One Unity Consciousness and to the Cosmic Logos: Avatar of Synthesis: the Mahatma.

Thank you, Beloved Ones. "And... So It Is!"

> The United Sacred Flames and Rays of Christed Light
> Consciousness – Image yourself within the core center of the
> Sacred Flames and Rays of Christed Light of God Consciousness,
> in Unity with Helios and Vesta of the Great Central Sun.

The United Twelve Sacred Flames and Rays –
The Sacred Flames of Christ Light Consciousness

Overlighted by: Helios and Vesta

Solar Council of Twelve

Lord Zohar of Shamballa

Cosmic Logos: Avatar of Synthesis: The Mahatma

Chohans: Maha Chohan and All Twelve
Chohans of the Flames and Rays

Archangel: Lord Metatron

Angelic Realm: Legions of Angels that Service the Flames and Rays

Key Attributes:

Solar Service: Solar Christ Consciousness, and the Reunion with
Helios and Vesta. The Combined Attributes of All the Sacred Flames
and Rays of Christed Light Consciousness lead to Unification, and
Oneness with the Christed Light Consciousness of the Holy Spirit.

Reunion with Helios and Vesta

Solar Service in Unification to Be All That Is;

Cosmic Logos: Avatar of Synthesis; the Mahatma!

Prayer to the Cosmic Logos: Avatar of Synthesis: the Mahatma

Beloved Holy One, the Ultimate and Supreme God of All Creations, the All That Is! The Beloved Cosmic Logos: Avatar of Synthesis, the Mahatma; the Maha Chohan and the Chohans of the Twelve Sacred Flames and Rays; the Archangels and the Divine Complements of the Twelve Sacred Flames and my Mighty I AM Presence to be present in this now moment.

I Feel the Sacred Flames and Rays Unite as One and enter into my Spirit, my Soul, my Heart, and all four Body Systems, Subtle Bodies, Body Elemental and Inner Child, to bring Healing, Love, Light, Inner Peace, Balance and Harmony to all levels of my being.

From the Sacred Chambers of my Heart, the United Sacred Flames and Rays connect me to the Christed Light of God Consciousness, the All That Is. I AM One, with the Heart, Mind and Will of God.

The United Sacred Flames and Rays connect All Humanity, All Kingdoms and Realms in and of the Earth to the Heart, Mind, and Will of God, The United Sacred Flames and Rays surround Mother Earth and Assist her in Ascending to the 5th Dimension and beyond, with ease and grace.

The Integrated Sacred Flames and Rays assist All on Planet Earth to Ascend to the 5th Dimension and beyond at this time, if they have chosen to do so.

I AM in Service to The One, the Ultimate and Supreme God of All Creations, and therefore know that this is for the Highest Good of All and for the Highest Good of the Universe.

I AM In Unity and Oneness, with the Heart, Mind and Will of God.

"And So It Is!"

Prayer to the Beloved Cosmic Logos: the Mahatma

Beloved Cosmic Logos: Avatar of Synthesis, the Mahatma. I Request that you Support me in embodying the appropriate and integrated vibrations of the United Twelve Sacred Flames and Rays of Light and Love.

Let their healing frequency heal my being and sustain the Crystalline Light already present, and expand the vibrations of The One, the Ultimate and Supreme God of All Creations that are held within the embodiment that is my being.

I AM the Embodiment of The One, and through this Acceptance and Purification process, I Receive with Gratitude all the Abundance that is provided to me from The One, the All That Is. I Embrace the Crystalline Light quotient levels within me and the Strengths of my Divine Inner Powers.

I Surrender to the Integration of the highest Divine Plans for me in this Now moment. I AM Receiving the gifts of my Highest Potentials through my Beloved Mighty I AM Presence. I Envision the Multi-colored Sacred Flames and Rays flowing over and through me. I Feel and Sense their Presence, and I Acknowledge their Beauty and Light.

I Embody the Integrated Energy as it flows through me. I Feel in Resonance and Harmony with the Energy of Abundance, Completeness and wholeness that the United Integrated Energy of the Sacred Flames and Rays bring unto me.

The United Sacred Flames and Rays of Cosmic Christed Light enhance my Gifts and Qualities with their Light Energies, and provide qualities within me that bring me to my Cosmic Ascension in the Light, be in alignment with my Life Purpose for this incarnation, and be for the Highest Light and Love in One Unity Consciousness. I AM the Embodiment of The One.

"And So It Is!"

Prayer to the United Integrated Twelve Sacred Flames and Rays

O Sacred Flames of Life on Earth, I AM in Gratitude and Love for your unending work in keeping our precious Mother Earth Alive.

I AM a Child of Earth and I AM Home to Rejoice in your Love. I AM once again united with the Children of the Inner Realms and the Inner Earth Cities of Infinite Wisdom and Love.

In Oneness and Unity with The One, the Ultimate and Supreme God of All Creations, the All That Is; In Oneness and Unity from my Heart, our Hearts become One Heart, Beating to the Rhythm of our Mother's Heart, The Hearts once broken and rendered apart are Now Rejuvenated, Revivified and Resurrected to their normal God-Self State.

Rejoice, Rejoice and Rejoice in Love and Light for Beloved Ones, I AM once again Free, and Restored to Divine Oneness and Unity with the Creator, The One, the Ultimate and Supreme God of All Creations, the All That Is.

My Journey of Cosmic Ascension continues United I AM and One with my God-Self State, Others and The One, the All That Is.

"And... So It Is!"

Invocation Prayer to the United Twelve Sacred Flames and Rays

The Invocation Prayer can be done for each Ray separately, and on their own day of the week. The energy for that day will amplify that Rays energy. (Invocation Prayer for Ray.......)

Ray 1. (Amplified Monday)

O Sacred Flame and Ray of the Will of God, I Surrender to you my Heart and Mind, to be in oneness with the Will of God. Beloved Blue Ray of Good Will, harness to you my Heart and Mind. Joyfully I surrender and reunite, with the Will of God Divine.
"And... So It Is!"

Ray 2. (Amplified Sunday)

O Sacred Flame and Ray of Illumination with your Yellow Rays, Illuminate my Mind and Heart to the Wisdom of the Mind of The One, the Supreme God of All Creation. The Divine Cosmic Mind opens my Mind to the ever-expanding Wisdom and Understanding of the Mind of God, to Higher Perspectives and to Christed Light of God Consciousness.
"And... So It Is!"

Ray 3. (Amplified Tuesday)

O Sacred Flame and Ray of Cosmic Love, Embrace my Heart with Compassion and Fill my Sacred Heart Chambers, with your Crystal Rose Pink Fire, the Essence of Divine Cosmic Love.
"And... So It Is!"

Ray 4. (Amplified Friday)

O Sacred Flame and Ray of Ascension and Purification,
Surround and Purify my Soul, my four Body Systems, all my
Subtle Energetic Bodies and the Body Elemental, with your pure
White Dazzling Flame of Ascension. Purify my entire being
of all negativity in preparation for the initiations to come.
"And... So It Is!"

Ray 5. (Amplified Wednesday)

O Sacred Flame and Ray of Healing and Manifestation,
Immerse my Soul, my four Body Systems, and all Subtle
Bodies into your Healing Flame. Blaze forth the Green
Emerald Light Essence of your Great Jade Fire and Heal all the
pain from my being to thereby, bring forth Transformation,
Abundance and Prosperity into my Life. "And... So It Is!"

Ray 6. (Amplified Thursday)

O Sacred Flame and Ray of Resurrection, with the Golden
Orange Healing Rays of your wondrous Fire, Rejuvenate and
Resurrect my Life and Heart to the God-Self State, Restore
to me my inherited Divinity and Perfection in preparation
for my Ascension to the 5th Dimension and Beyond.
"And... So It Is!"

Ray 7. (Amplified Saturday)

O Sacred Flame and Ray of Transmutation, the Violet Flame
of St. Germain Encapsulate my Heart, my Soul, my four Body
Systems, all my Subtle Energetic Bodies and the Body Elemental
with waves upon waves of the Violet Flame, to Transmute and
Transform all negative energy and programs to the positive
energy of Freedom, Forgiveness and Unconditional Love.
"And... So It Is!"

Ray 8. (Amplified Wednesday)

O Sacred Flame and Ray of Transcendence, Immerse me with your Aqua Sea/Green Flame of Certainty and Clarity, So that I AM Clear and Concise in my thoughts and emotions. Thus, I Transcend All concerns that lead to confusion and indecision.
"And... So It Is!"

Ray 9. (Amplified Tuesday)

O Sacred Flame and Ray of Highest Potentials, Surround me with the Energy of my Gifts, Encapsulated with waves upon waves of your magenta fire, bringing to me the Divine Attributes of the Synthesis of Rays 1 to 7 so that these are manifested in my Life in this now moment of time.
"And... So It Is!"

Ray 10. (Amplified Monday)

O Sacred Flame and Ray of Divinity and Peace, Shower me with your Pearlescent Fire to clear away all that which is impure and not of the Divine energy of The One, the Ultimate, Supreme God of All Creation. Let there be peace in my Spirit, Soul, Heart and Mind, as I Release unto the Flame and Ray of Divinity all that which serves me not. I AM in the Peace of my Beloved Monad, and my Mighty I AM Presence.
"And... So It Is!"

Ray 11. (Amplified on Thursday)

O Sacred Flame and Ray of Illumine Truth, your Wisdom I do adore, Sacred Peach Flame and Ray of Illumine Truth Immerse my entire being into your Flame, so that I AM Embraced by your essence of Joy and Serenity in the Truth of the Knowledge of Who I AM as I AM the embodiment the energy of The One, the All That Is.
"And... So It Is!"

Ray 12. (Amplified on Sunday)

O Sacred Flame and Ray of Oneness, the Sacred Golden Flame
and Ray of One Unity Consciousness, as I Seek to be in Oneness
within my Spiritual God-Self, I Call upon you to shower me with
the Golden Flame and Ray of Transfiguration, so that all energies
held within me are Transfigured to the Oneness and Wellness
of One Unity Consciousness with The One, the All That Is.
"And... So It Is!"

Ray 13. (Amplified Daily)

O Sacred Flames and Rays of Harmony, United in Oneness, you swirl
your energies into a vortex of wondrous Healing Powers that encompass
all the attributes of all the Sacred Flames and Rays and as you integrate
and balance, you bring Peace, Harmony and Tranquillity. I AM One
with my Spiritual God-Self State and I AM One with the Beloved One,
the Ultimate and Supreme God of All Creations, the All That Is.
I AM One with the Sacred Cosmic Flames and Rays.
"And... So It Is!"

Prayer: I AM the Master of My Destiny

My Beloved Mighty I AM Presence, Lord God essence of my being; I AM in the Mastery of my Destiny. I Rejoice, Rejoice, Rejoice in my abilities to resolve and dissolve all negative energies, thought forms and emotions, as they appear to me and as shown by Spirit and from my Soul – the Holy Spirit God-Self State that I AM.

As the Master of my Destiny, I Choose to remove all negativity from my four Body Systems. I Send all negativity to the Light of Source, which is at the central core of my Sacred Heart, for resolution and to be dissolve by the Transmutation, Transformation and Transfiguration Flames and Rays of the Sacred Christed Light of God Consciousness, which are within the Sacred Gateways and Portals of my Heart, connecting me to the Truth of Who I AM as a Master of Light and Love.

All my Past Life Akashic Records have been Cleared and Cleansed of any and all Imbalances, and Restored to the Divine Perfection of Balance and Harmony.

All Memories and Records that are held in my Subconscious Mind have been Cleared and Cleansed, and Restored to the Perfection of the Christed Light of God Consciousness.

All Beliefs, Patterns and Programs contained within my Conscious Mind, my Subconscious Mind, and my Super Conscious Mind are Reframed, Restored and Resurrected to the Light and Love of the Cosmic Heart and Mind of God.

I AM Living from the Sacred Chambers of my
Heart, as the Master that I AM.
"And... So It Is!"

Prayer to Archangel Lord Metatron
of the Angelic Realm

Beloved Archangel Lord Metatron of the Angelic Realm, in all that you do and in all that you hold, I AM in Gratitude to you from the very depths of my Soul. I Honor you and your beingness with all that I AM.

I See, Hear and Feel in all that surrounds me the Light Energy that is you. I Feel Blessed in the knowing that the All That Is also is you.

I know with every fibre of my being that we are One. As a child of The One, I emulate you in my Breath, in my Thoughts and Emotions, and in my Soul.

I AM Grateful for all that you are in my Life; As you walk with me throughout my Life, I Feel your Presence within me. You Guide me and show me by your example, the way home to be in Unity with my God-Self, to be in Unity with others, and to be in Unity with The One, the Ultimate and Supreme God of All Creations, the All That Is;

I AM One with my God-Self. I AM One with Others. I AM One with You Archangel Metatron.

I AM One with the One, I AM All That Is.
"And... So It Is!"

> The Sacred Cosmic Rays of Light – Image yourself within a Circle
> of Cosmic Light Rays and at the core center of the Sacred Rays,
> feel immersed with them and traverse these Rays to the Portals
> and the Gateways to all Dimensions of Time and Space.

Cosmic Prayers

Prayer of the Portal of Diamonds

I have no other journey Only the One within myself;

As I Pass through the Portal of Diamonds,

And bathe in the Splendor of My Glorious Mighty I AM Presence,

I know that the Cosmic Heart of The One, the All That Is,

Blesses me with Unconditional Love and Christed Light,

And with the Blessings from the Cosmic Heart,

Coming through me as a sparkling River of Diamonds,

Bringing Peace, Love and Harmony to All,

I AM That I AM,

I AM the Diamond Heart, the All That Is!

I AM my True Self, the Holy God-Self of my Diamond Heart!

"And... So It Is!"

Prayer to the Cosmic Rays of Light

O Cosmic Rays of Light, Surround my Heart and Mind with
Enlightenment, Awareness and Harmony. Light up the Sacred
Chambers of My Heart and Mind with your Crystal Clear Diamond
Fire of All-Knowing and Cosmic Understanding of All That Is.
O Cosmic Rays of Light, the Diamond Fire that is your
Portal, the Gateway to all Dimensions of Time and Space,
Embrace me with your Enlightenment and Acceptance that
I AM Worthy to pass through your Cosmic Gateways. I AM
Purity in One United Consciousness with All That Is.
I AM One with the Cosmic Rays.
I AM that I AM!
"And... So It Is!"

Prayer of Connection to the Planetary Crystalline Grid

My Beloved Mighty I AM Presence, Lord God essence of my being, be within me now as I Call upon the Beloved Planetary Hierarchy, Beloved Universal Hierarchy, and the Beloved Planetary Goddess: Gaia/Virgo the sentient being Mother of Earth. I AM That I AM. Connect me with the Crystalline Grids that Surrounds Planet Earth. I AM of Pure Intent and my Heart's Desire is to connect to these Crystalline Grids. I AM Dedicated in my Service to Planet Earth.

I Desire for Planet Earth: Perfection in Health and the Removal of all negative energies that cause disharmony to the Planet. I Request that all the negative energies in their removal be Transmuted to the positive energies of Freedom, Forgiveness and Unconditional Love, and be used for the Healing and Transformation of Planet Earth to Cosmic Christed Light of God Consciousness.

I AM a Crystalline Child of God. I Desire for Planet Earth to achieve Comic Ascension to the 5th Dimension, in ease and grace. I AM in Gratitude for the Opportunity to be of Service to the Mother in her Cosmic Ascension. I Ask that her Cosmic Ascension be achieved in Ease and Grace and be for the Highest Good of all.

I AM in my Heart Energy, Committed and in Oneness with all beings of Light that are connected to the Crystalline Grids of Planet Earth, to bring about that which is for the greatest good of all. My Heart Energy is One with the Heart of Lemuria. I AM in One Unity Consciousness with Planet Earth. I Create in the Physical, through the process of Crystallization, a World that is Harmonious, Balanced and Peaceful, One that resides in the Heart Energy of the Crystalline Grid.

I AM That I AM. I Reach into the Hearts and Minds of All who are connected with the Crystalline Grid. I Desire for ALL to be Awakened and Aware of the Unconditional Love of The One, and the Oneness and Unity Consciousness that is All That Is.

Blessings of Love and Light to All! "For this
I Give Thanks, And... So It Is!"

Prayer to the Cosmic Rays for Peace and Harmony

Oh Beloved One, the Ultimate and Supreme God of All Creations. Manifest for this World, Planet Earth, in this Very Moment of the Now, The Wondrous Peace, Harmony and Unconditional Love, that is the birth right of All the Children of God.

Send forth the Cosmic Rays to impart unto All the Kingdoms and Realms of Planet Earth, the Knowledge that you are Unconditional Love. Your Love is Eternal and Bestowed upon All of your Children – regardless of Religion, Race, Creed or Species – and includes All the Kingdoms and Realms of Planet Earth.

Beloved One, the Ultimate and Supreme God of All Creations, I Claim my birth right as a Child of your Creation, the Peace, Harmony, Love, Compassion and Mercy, the Love and Light of the Christed Light of God Consciousness, that you ordained was for all of your Children. As in Heaven... so it is on Earth.

O Beloved One, the Ultimate and Supreme God of All Creations, the All That Is, Create in this very Now moment of time, Heaven on Planet Earth, Surrounding and Permeating All with the Holy Spirit, the Cosmic Rays of the Christed Light of God Consciousness.

Peace and Harmony I AM!
"And... So It Is!"

Prayer to the Cosmic Platinum Ray
of Purification, Light and Love

Cosmic Platinum Ray of Purification, Light and Love, Come in with your Ray of Purification, and Restore All the Land and Water Regions of Planet Earth to Optimum Health and Well-being.

Cosmic Platinum Ray of Purification, Light and Love, Rejuvenate the arid drought-affected lands of the World. Restore and Regenerate the water ways to vibrant Life Force Energy. Manifest the removal of all that which is harmful and Detrimental to their Rebirth and Regenerative growth; Restore and Rejuvenate All the Lands and Waterways of Planet Earth to Optimum Health and Well-being.

Cosmic Platinum Ray of Purification, Light and Love, awaken All of Humanity to their responsibilities as Caretakers of Planet Earth and the awareness of the Goddess Gaia/Virgo, our Beloved Mother of Earth and to our Duty as Custodians of her Well-being.

Cosmic Platinum Ray of Purification, Light and Love, Restore to the Heart, Mind and Will of Humanity the knowledge that they are to be in Oneness with Mother Nature, All Life Forms and All Life Force Energy, that dwells here on Planet Earth. And to Command the respect of Humanity toward Mother Earth in order that All Life forms and All Life Force Energy, All the Kingdoms and Realms of Earth Is sustained and maintained in accordance with the Universal Laws of Purification and Ascension; Peace and Harmony I AM. I AM in Self-responsibility, therefore, upon the completion of my healing and the manifestation of my Purification, Self- Love and Enlightenment. I Let Go and Release the Cosmic Platinum Ray back to the Source of All That Is.

I Request that all Restoration and Rejuvenation is done in Ease and Grace, and be for the Highest Good of Planet Earth and the Highest Good of the Universe.

"I AM in Gratitude and I AM Thankful. And ... So It Is!"

Prayer to the Platinum Ray

Beloved Platinum Ray; I Feel you in my life, and I Embrace the many influences that you bring. I AM in Gratitude for your coming. I embody all that you are teaching me in my Journey of Cosmic Ascension to the 5th Dimension and beyond. My Mighty I AM Presence and you the Platinum Ray are One within me, and as you enter my being; all my thoughts and feelings are Purified to Balance and Harmony, Love and Light, Truth and Integrity, and the All-Knowing that I AM the Master of My Destiny, and a Master in My Ascension.

I AM at Peace; my Mind, Body, Spirit and Soul, Embody the Purification energy of the Platinum Ray within the Sacred Chambers of My Heart. I Feel the Integrity and the Truth of the Platinum Ray as it touches my Core Issues and Problems. I Accept the Truth as being my True-Self my God-Self, expressing its Truth, the Truth of who I AM, through the Power of the Platinum Ray.

I Feel the Regenerative Power of the Platinum Ray as it restores my Physical and Etheric Bodies to Perfect Health, reactivating the Crystalline Body of my Self Mastery. My Twelve Strand DNA is reactivated. My Physical and Etheric Bodies experience a complete transformation and regeneration as is appropriate for my evolution.

I Release all Struggle and Resistance of this Truth to the Platinum Ray and in so doing, know the Inner Peace and Harmony of The One, the Ultimate and Supreme Mind of God.

I Surrender my Limiting Beliefs of how I Believe things ought to be for my life, and for the lives of others, to the Sword of the Platinum Ray – to be converted to the Truth, Integrity and Purity of the Christed Light of God Consciousness contained within the Sword.

I AM in Acceptance of the Purification and the Truth as they are shown to me and thus I AM Freedom, I AM Purity, I AM Truth, I AM Integrity and I AM Peaceful in All Situations. As I feel the God-Power Spirit within me; and I AM in Acceptance of God's Plan for my Life.

I Let Go and Let God Control my Life. And as I Go with the Flow, All is in Ease and Grace. I AM Grateful to the Universal Logos: Lord Melchizedek, and the Order of Melchizedek for the manifestation of the magnificent Platinum Ray to Planet Earth.

I AM in Self-responsibility; therefore, upon the completion of my healing, the manifestation of my optimum health, I Let Go and Release the Platinum Ray back to the Source of All That Is.

"I AM in Gratitude and I AM Thankful. And ... So It Is!"

Invocation to the Twin Rays of the Divine Feminine and the Divine Masculine – (for Justice, Equality, Support and Abundance for All)

Beloved One, the Ultimate and Supreme God of All Creation, the All That Is! Beloved Cosmic Logos: the Avatar of Synthesis; the Mahatma. Beloved Universal Logos: Lord Melchizedek and the Beloved Planetary Logos: Lord Gautama Buddha.

The Divine Feminine and the Divine Masculine Principles within me are joined in Oneness of Spirit, Harmony and Unconditional Love; we are God-Power in Action. I AM in Oneness with my Divine Twin Flame, my Divine I AM Presence is in Oneness with my Divine Twin Flame.

My Twin Flame and I are United and in Oneness with each other in Spirit, and our mighty Monads are within us now. My Twin Flame and I have One Heart, One Mind and One Will, The One, the Ultimate and Supreme God of All Creation is within us now.

I AM that I AM a Child of God and I AM One with the All That Is. I AM Supported and Abundant in All things and in All areas of my Life. I AM Supported by The One, the Ultimate and Supreme God of All Creation, in All that I Do.

I AM Living my Life in the Truth, Justice and Transparency. I Trust in the Support and Fairness of The One, the Ultimate and Supreme God of All That Is.

I Hereby affirm that the Cosmic Laws of Justice apply to All Life Forms and All Life Force energies within this Cosmic All.

The vibrations and frequencies of Transparency and Integrity in All things – Respect and Responsibility toward others, the Support and Fair distribution of God's Abundance to All – flowing through to Unconditional Love, Fairness, Equality; Compassion, Mercy, Metaphysical and Physical

Laws are Distributed to All Life Forms and All Life Force energies, in accordance with the New Encodements for the Cosmic All.

The New Encodements of Divine Perfection in All things, as per the Holy-Spirit Consciousness of The One, the Ultimate and Supreme God of All Creations.

The Divine Feminine and The Divine Masculine Principles are United and in Oneness. The Twin Flame energies are United and in Oneness with each other.

Balance, Harmony and Equilibrium are Cosmic Laws, applied to All Levels of Creation, whatsoever their Life Source energy – be they of the Light or the Dark.

All Energies that reside in the Cosmic All shall abide by the Cosmic Laws of Justice, Truth, Equality of Support and Freedom in Evolution, secure from any interference whatsoever from the Metaphysical and Physical Realms.

By Cosmic Law and Decree; All Life Forms and All Life Force energies forthwith, are to Respect and not interfere in the Spiritual/Soul or Physical Growth of others, another Life Form or Life Force energy.

It is stated herein, that the development and evolution of All Life Forms and All Life Force energies, in this Cosmic All, are the Jurisdiction of the Elohim Council of Elders and the Cosmic Logos: the Avatar of Synthesis; the Mahatma, and are done in accordance with the Holy Writ for the New Encodements of Divine Perfection as declared by The One, the Ultimate and Supreme God of All Creations.

I AM in Gratitude for the Wisdom, Justice and Unconditional Love for All Life, irrespective of the Life Form or Life Force energies as shown by the Divine Feminine and the Divine Masculine Principles.

I AM Eternally Grateful for the Unconditional Love and Dispensations from The One, the All That Is.

I AM Humble and I AM One with All.

"And... So It Is!"

Prayer to Master Adama of Telos

Beloved Master Adama, High Priest of Telos and the Telosian Council of Elders; Beloved Masters and Lady Masters of the Temples for the Sacred Flames in Telos; the Archangels and their Divine Complements; and all members of the Galactic Federation residing in Telos, in this now moment.

I AM here this day in the Temple of my Heart, the Sacred Chambers of my Heart. I AM Open to receive from you the Blessings of Love and Harmony that are the energies of Telos, and all my Brothers and Sisters who are in Telos and within the Telos Communities, around the World.

I AM in Deepest Gratitude for your Unconditional Love and the Light of Harmony that you are in bringing to me this day, the wonders of your Wisdom, Understanding and Truth. I AM in Deepest Gratitude for the Teachings that you have personally delivered to us – your family upon the surface of this Beautiful Planet, our Home; Mother Earth.

I AM in Deepest Gratitude for your Presence in the Earth – for Mother Earth, Humanity and All the Kingdoms of Earth. I thank you from the Sacred Chambers of my Heart to your Hearts, for the Divine Service that you have been to The One, the Ultimate and Supreme God of All Creations.

I AM Open to be with you and for you to be with me in this NOW moment. I Kneel before the Alter of my Heart in Worship to the Cosmic Light of Christ. I Receive an Infusion of Light from the Great Central Sun. With this Infusion of Light I AM in my own reunification. I AM connected with the Divinity That I AM, and the Great Plan of Light that is my Beloved I AM Presence.

I AM Open in the Sacred Chambers of my Heart to Embrace the Massive Energies of Transformation as they come to me, with ease and grace. I Feel your Embrace and my Entire beingness is Encapsulated with the Energies of Unconditional Love and Harmony – that is Lemurian, the Heart of Lemuria.

I AM in profound humbleness, as I AM in awareness of the Service that you are and image to us all, and I AM as you are, a devoted servant to the All That Is, The One, the Ultimate and Supreme God of All Creations.

"I AM in One Unity Consciousness Now!
And So It Is!"

Prayer to Lord Zohar of Shamballa

Beloved Lord Zohar of the Sacred Flame and Ray of Harmony, in Gratitude and Wonder, I Feel the Wisdom and Understanding of your Light and Love. With ease and grace, I Embody the Sacred Flame and Ray of Harmony within my Sacred Heart and Sacred Soul.

As I gaze upon the Sacred Flame and Ray of Harmony, I Feel the Resonance in my Sacred Heart, which vibrates with the expanded frequency of Harmony, Love and Compassion toward my Spirit, my Soul, my Body Elemental, and my Inner Child, to All of Humanity and All the Kingdoms and Realms of Mother Earth.

My Spirit, Soul, Heart, Mind, Emotions and Physical Body vibrate to the frequency of the Sacred Flame and Ray of Harmony. I Embrace and Embody the Equilibrium Energy of the Sacred Flame and Ray. I AM in Acceptance of Everything as it is and what it is: Divine Perfection, Balance and Harmony.

I Open myself to be of Service to the Divine Principles of Harmony. I AM a Keeper of the attributes of Harmony. I acknowledge that you Lord Zohar, the Masters and Lady Masters of the Sacred Flame of Harmony, and the Divine Angels of Harmony are with me and Guide me through the many levels of Harmony and Acceptance: Until I AM That I AM, in complete and total Acceptance of All Things in their Divine Perfection of Balance and Harmony.

I Choose to be in Acceptance of Who I AM, and to be in Acceptance of ALL others and who they are, as we are all Divine Perfection in One Unity Consciousness with our Holy Christed God-Self. I AM the Embodiment of the Sacred Flame and Ray of Harmony. I AM the Embodiment of Balance, Peace and Tranquillity. I AM the Embodiment of the Holy Spirit within my Sacred Heart. I AM the Embodiment of Harmony, in my Heart, my Mind, my Spirit and my Soul.

In Gratitude I AM Harmony. I AM That I AM. "And... So It Is!"

Prayer for Harmony

My Beloved Might I AM Presence, Lord God of my being, I Ask for the Blessings of the Flame of Harmony to be within me always.

I Strive to Remain in the State of Harmony at all times. As I do so, I AM Living in Harmony with All of Creation and All of Nature.

I AM Harmony in All Situations, blessing all beings that come into my life as I Go Forth with what is my own Truth, the truth of my Mighty I AM Presence.

I Remain where Harmony reigns at all times in the NOW moment. I Surround myself in the Total Acceptance of what is.

I AM a Seeker of Illumine Truth and Harmony. I Embrace the New Energies that are flooding the Earth with all of my Heart, Mind, Body and Soul.

I AM in Total Acceptance of Who I AM and what I have been. I Strive always to improve myself. I AM in Deepest Gratitude for all the Assistance that I AM Receiving in this now moment.

I AM Harmony and Harmony is the number one quality in my Life that I Embody. As I Live in Harmony, it paves the way for my admittance to the "Hall of Ascension."

I AM in my Heart always. I AM in Gratitude and I AM Happy with All of Creation. In Total Acceptance of What Is, I See the Perfection in All Things and in All Situations.

I AM Receiving the Blessings of the Flame of Harmony Now! I AM in Gratitude for the Sacred Flame of Harmony. I AM in Deepest Gratitude to Lord Zohar, Lord of the Sacred Flame and Ray of Harmony

Blessed I AM! "And... So It Is!"

Prayer for Peace on Earth, Good Will toward All Humanity

Beloved One, the Ultimate and Supreme God of All Creations, the All That Is! Beloved Cosmic Logos: Avatar of Synthesis: the Mahatma. The Universal Logos: Lord Melchizedek. The Universal Judge; Galactic Logos: Lord Melchior. Helios and Vesta of the Great Central Sun. Beloved Planetary Logos: Lord Gautama Buddha. Beloved Lord Sanat Kumara and Lady Venus: Lord Zohar of Shamballa and the Beloved Planetary Christ: Lord Maitreya.

I Desire with all of my Sacred Heart, Spirit, Soul, Mind and Might for Peace on Earth and Good Will toward all Humanity through and from the Cosmic Heart, Mind and Will of God.

The Full Divine Intervention of the Godforce has been called forth, to manifest Peace and Harmony through the Energy of the Cosmic Christed Light of God Consciousness and Cosmic Love, Wisdom and Understanding of The One, the Ultimate and Supreme God of All Creations, into the troubled Regions of Planet Earth, in this now moment of time.

I Decree with all my Sacred Heart, Spirit, Soul, Mind and Might, that God's Divine Plan of Peace and Harmony for Planet Earth is now manifested, Anchored, Activated, Actualized and Amplified; Into all Governments of all Nations on Planet Earth, All World and United Nations Corporations and Into the Earth, Air and Water Areas and Regions of Planet Earth.

I Thank you and I accept this as being done for the Highest Good of All and in Accordance with Divine Will of God, in the Divine Perfection of All That Is,

"And... So It Is!"

Prayer to the Spirit of Mount Shasta

Mountain of Wonder, Master of Mystery, impart unto me the Mysteries within thee.

Mountain of Wonder, Master of Teaching, impart unto me the Teachings within thee.

Mountain of Wonder, Master of Stillness, impart unto me the Stillness within thee.

Mountain of Wonder, Master of Gateways, impart unto me the Gateways within thee.

Mountain of Wonder, Master of Challenges, impart unto me the Challenges within thee.

Mountain of Wonder, Master of Wisdom, impart unto me the Wisdom within thee.

Mountain of Wonder, Master of Courage, impart unto me the Courage within thee.

Mountain of Wonder, Master of Light, impart unto me the Light within thee.

Mountain of Wonder, Master of Love, impart unto me the Love within thee.

Mountain of Wonder, Master of Life, impart unto me the Life within thee.

Mountain of Wonder, Master of Peace, impart unto me the Peace within thee.

Mountain of Wonder, Master of Reflection, impart unto me the Reflections within thee.

Mountain of Wonder, Master of Oneness, impart unto me the Oneness within thee

Mountain of Wonder, Master of Christed Light, impart unto me the Christed Light within thee.

Mountain of Wonder, impart unto me the Wonder that is thee.

"And... So It Is!"

Prayer for Planet Earth's Cosmic Ascension

I Call upon the Beloved One, the Ultimate and Supreme God of All Creations. Beloved Elohim Council of Co-Creator Gods; the Beloved Cosmic Hierarchy and Cosmic Logos: Avatar of Synthesis; the Mahatma. The Universal Hierarchy and Universal Logos: Lord Melchizedek. Planetary Logos: Lord Gautama Buddha. Beloved Planetary Hierarchy and the Planetary Christ: Lord Maitreya.

The Great White Brotherhood and the Company of Heaven that are the Christed Light of God Consciousness of this Universe and the Cosmic All to Anchor, Activate, Actualize and Amplify all the points of the Planetary Crystalline Grid of Planet Earth, to connect with the corresponding points of the Crystalline Grid of the Great Central Sun of this Universe.

I Decree that Planet Earth is Resurrected to the New Encodements of Divine Perfection as per the Universal Laws of One Unity Consciousness. I Decree that Planet Earth is lifted through the Veils of Consciousness, Resurrected and Aligned within the Universe, and Embodies the Universal Laws of Christed Light of God Consciousness.

I Decree that this Universe is lifted through the Higher Levels of Consciousness and Resurrected and Aligned to the Cosmic Laws and to the Cosmic Light of Christed Light of God Consciousness. I Decree that this is God's Will for Planet Earth and for the Universe. God's Will is done, God's Will is done, God's Will is done. And So It Is!

Planet Earth is Resurrected to her Rightful Place in space, Finite and Infinite, Oneness and Unity, Light and Love. The Universe is Resurrected to its Rightful Place in space, Finite and Infinite, Oneness and Unity, Cosmic Light and Cosmic Love.

God's Grace is upon Planet Earth, and with all beings that dwell therein forever.

Beloved I AM! Thank You! Thank You! Thank You! "And... So It Is!"

Prayer for Guidance

My Beloved Teachers and Guides, as I sit here in this glorious place and I ponder the wonder of what has been presented to me in Life, I have felt challenged by the many messages that have come through from you my Divine Teachers and Guides and my Mighty I AM Presence – the who and what I AM and why I AM here in this lifestream at this time.

I AM not so challenged by these messages as I once was, and in how the messages come forth from you – through my Heart, my Mind and my Body.

I Ask you for your assistance in clearing the remaining levels of doubt and resistance, and for the Cleansing Rays of the Christed Light, the Cosmic Light of Knowledge, Wisdom and Understanding and the Healing Rays of the Emerald Fire and the Resurrection Flame, to absorb all negative energies stored within my being, which are held on all levels of my four Body Systems, so that these negative energies cease to exist, and are Transmuted, Transformed and Transfigured to Peace, Balance, Harmony and Unconditional Love.

I Recognize that my Conscious and Unconscious Minds are Cleansed and Purified of all negative energies. I Have Received the Wisdom and Understanding that I Required so that these Energies are now Relinquished to the Cosmic Christed Light.

I Know that you will do whatever is for my Highest Good and the Highest Good of All. I have the Forbearance, Fortitude and Courage to Rise to the Challenges and to do Honor unto my Service to The One, the Ultimate and Supreme God of All Creations, the All That Is. I AM Empowered on all levels of my being. I have fulfilled all tasks that are asked of me in accordance with Gods Heart, Gods Mind and Gods Will.

Thy Will is Done! Thy Will is Done! Thy Will is Done! In Gratitude I Thank You.

"And... So It Is!"

Prayer for Guiding Light and Love

Guiding Light of my Beloved Mighty I AM Presence, bring forth the Cosmic Light and Cosmic Love of the Christed Light of God Consciousness, to change all the vibrations and frequencies energies held within my being, across all levels and dimensions of time and space, to be Cleansed and Cleared of all that is not Purity.

All the Energy that I have been, as part of my Evolutional Journey, has been Restored to Unconditional Love, Wisdom and Understanding, Balance, Harmony, Peace and Oneness.

All the hurt and harm that I have caused to myself and to others has been Healed by the Cosmic Light and Cosmic Love of the Christed Light of God Consciousness.

All the hurt and harm that I have received from others, has been healed by the Cosmic Light and Cosmic Love of the Christed Light of God Consciousness.

Guiding Light and Love of my Beloved Mighty I AM Presence, brings forth the Unconditional Love of the Holy God Energy, the Christed Light of God Consciousness, so that my broken Heart is Healed, and Restore to Optimum Health.

The energies held within my being, across all levels and dimensions of time and space are Purified, Healed and Blessed by the Unconditional Love of God.

I AM Light! I AM Love! I AM All That Is! I AM That I Am!
Thank You, Thank You, Thank You. I AM This I AM.
"And... So It Is!"

Prayer for the Miracle of Manifestation

My Beloved Mighty I AM Presence, please take me each night to the Temples of the Twelve Sacred Flames and Rays of Christed Light of God Consciousness, so that I AM prepared for the initiations I AM to Receive. I Ask to be prepared fully for the Dimensional Gateways that are Open to me. I Ask the Mother Earth Energy to receive and balance my Energy Fields and prepare my Physical, Spiritual, Mental and Emotional being for my Ascending the Mountain within, with ease and grace.

I Ask the Inner Mountain Energy to embrace me and carry me in my Journey to the Pinnacle of the Mount. I Call upon my Beloved Mighty I AM Presence to take me to the Temple of the Whales, so that I may Communicate with the Ancient Ones and be blessed by their Wisdom

I Request that my Spirit, Soul and my four Body Systems are prepared for this greater wisdom and the Opening of my Higher Heart and Thymus, my Pineal and Pituitary Glands of the Brain. Beloved Mighty I AM Presence, I Request the Miracle of my Ascension to the 5th Dimension and Beyond to be in my Life as soon as I meet all requirements. I Ask for all initiation procedures to take place and be for my highest good and the highest good of the Planet Earth and the Universe.

The Miracle of Prosperity and Financial Freedom is to be made Manifest in my Life Now! The Miracle of Unconditional Love in all my Relationships – with Self, Others and the Universe – is made Manifest in my Life, and also that which is for my Highest Good and the Highest Good of all.

The Miracle of Perfect Health to be made Manifest in my Life and is in accordance with the Divine Plan for my Life and Life Purpose, being for my Highest Good and the Highest Good of All. The Miracle of the Violet Flame resides within me and around me on all levels of my being, across all dimensions of time and space, 24 hours a day, 7 days a week. The Miracles of my Life are made Manifest Now! I AM Eternally Grateful for the Miracle of Manifestation. "And... So It Is!"

An Advanced Healing Meditation
Treatment Prayer

Prayer to the Holy Spirit of Cosmic Christed Light Consciousness

My Beloved Mighty I AM Presence, Lord God Essence of my being, through you I Call upon the Beloved Planetary Logos: Lord Gautama Buddha. Planetary Hierarchy: Lord Sanat Kumara and Lady Venus. The Planetary Christ: Lord Maitreya. Universal Logos: Lord Melchizedek. Beloved Maha Chohan: Master St. Germain and the Chohans of the Twelve Sacred Flames and Rays of Christed Light of God Consciousness.

I Call upon you to witness my request to the Holy Spirit of the Cosmic Christed Light of God Consciousness. I AM my Mighty I AM Presence and I Invoke the Holy Spirit of the Cosmic Christed Light of God Consciousness to enter my Spirit and Soul, and all levels of my beingness – to come down through the Layers of my Multiverses Self, my Universal Self and my Multi-dimensional Self, God-Self, entering my Auric Fields, all levels of my Auric Sheathes, through the Etheric Field, my Chakra System, Meridian System and into my Physical Body and Body Elemental, connecting with the Crystalline Mother Lode energy of Mother Earth.

I AM my Mighty I AM Presence and I Invoke the Holy Spirit of the Cosmic Christed Light of God Consciousness to enter my Physical Being, my Body Elemental, the Cellular Structure of my Body, to encapsulate every Atom, Proton, Electron and Neutron of my Body with the Healing Powers of the Cosmic Christed Light of The Holy Spirit. Healing with Unconditional Love and Light, all levels of my being, across all dimensions, Universes and Multiverses.

I AM my Mighty I AM Presence. I Invoke the Holy Spirit of the Cosmic Christed Light of God Consciousness to pass through and around every Neutron, Electron, Proton, Atom and the Cellular Structure of my Body, with the Healing Powers of the Cosmic Christed Light of The Holy Spirit, moving through my Body Elemental, embracing my Body Elemental with Unconditional Love and Light, passing out through my Chakra System, Meridian System, Etheric Field and all the Auric Sheathes that surround my Body, my Spiritual God-Self, my Soul, returning to the Cosmos, through my Multi-dimensional Self, Universal Self and Multiverses Self. To finally return to the One Unity Consciousness of the Holy Spirit of the Cosmic Christed Light of God Consciousness.

I AM my Mighty I AM Presence. I Command that this is done in accordance with the Holy Writ for my Life, and that this is for my Highest Good and the Highest Good of all.

Thy Will is Done, Thy Will is Done, Thy Will is Done Now!
Beloved Holy Spirit that I AM! "And... So It Is!"

Prayer for Cosmic Christed Light Healing

I Invoke the Sacred Flames and Rays of Christed Light of God Consciousness to come in to permeate and saturate every Particle, Cell, Atom, Proton, Electron and Neutron of my being, to Transform, Transmute and Transfigure all the Energy that had been contained and accumulated within all levels of my beingness, to the Cosmic Light and Cosmic Love of Freedom, Forgiveness, Unconditional Love, Wisdom, Understanding and the One Unity Consciousness of The One, the Ultimate and Supreme God of All Creation, the All That Is.

"And... So It Is!"

Prayer to Release and Relinquish to the Divine Light of Source

I Release and Relinquish to the Divine Light of Source, the All That Is, all negative energies contained within my being, my Spirit, my Soul, Mind/Emotion, Etheric, Physical Body, Body Elemental and Inner Child, that have kept me in pain and trauma.

I Release and Relinquish to the Divine Light of Source, the All That Is, the Akashic Records of all my Past Lives, that I have ever lived, including this current life incarnation, that all the negative energies that stem from events and incidence of the past be Restored to Peace, Balance, Harmony, Unconditional Love, Freedom and Forgiveness.

I Release and Relinquish to the Divine Light of Source, the All That Is, All the Drama and Stories that are held within my Unconscious Mind, and Super Conscious Mind, so that I AM Living Free and I AM Forgiven for all the beliefs of transgressions against myself and toward others that I have held within my beingness.

I Invoke the United Twelve Sacred Flames and Rays of Christed Light of God Consciousness to Transmute, Transform and Transfigure all meanings, beliefs, patterns and programs contained within my Mind/Emotions and Physical Body, to the New Encodements of Divine Perfection that is the Love of God.

Love Is All That Is!
"And... So It Is!"

Prayer to Release Past Life Incarnation Records (a releasing prayer)

Beloved Mighty I AM Presence, my Beloved Higher Self, and the Beloved Lords of Karma, the Universal Judge, and the Universal Logos: Lord Melchizedek.

I Release and Relinquish unto you all Akashic Records pertaining to my Past Life Incarnations and my Current Life here on Earth and of elsewhere in this Universe, to be Cleared and Cleansed of All that which Serves me not, in this now moment of time.

I Command that all levels of meanings, beliefs, patterns and programs, be shown to me for the Wisdom and Understanding that they contain, and that they are Transformed, and Transfigured to Balance and Harmony of the Feminine and Masculine Principles.

I Release and Relinquish unto the Universal Light of Source, which I embody within the Sacred Chambers of my Heart, all negative energies, beliefs, patterns and programs of Lack: Lack of Prosperity, Health, Loving Relationships, Confidence, Assertiveness, Self-Doubt, Self-Belief, Self-Worth, Self-Esteem, Self-Value, Sexuality and Self-Acceptance.

Fear: Fear of Deprivation, Betrayal, Self-Sabotage, Self-Destructiveness, Victimization, Violence, Aggression, De-validations, Sexual and Physical Abuse.

I Release and Relinquish all Mental and Emotional issues pertaining to: Procrastination, Interruptions, Interventions, Interference, Entitlement, Resentment, Hesitation, Aloneness, Separation from Self and Others, Impatience, Self-Injustice, Self-Judgement, Self-Criticism and Self-Denial of the Truth of Who I AM, my True God-Self.

I Transmute, Transform and Transfigure all my negative causal belief patterns to positive causal belief patterns, eliminating the old negative causal beliefs by embracing NEW positive causal beliefs that shift my Energy to Higher Levels of Consciousness.

I Release and Let Go of the Frustration, Anger and Resentment Energies that all these old beliefs, patterns, programs, issues and problems bring to the surface of my Conscious Mind, from my Unconscious Mind, my Super Consciousness and my Cellular Memory.

I Let Go of and Clear to the Universal Source of Light all Stories and Dramas from my Conscious Mind, my Unconscious Mind, my Super Consciousness, my Cellular Memory, my Body Elemental's Memory Bank and all my Past Lives.

I Retain within my being, only that which serves me in the undertaking of my Mission Purpose here on Planet Earth and in this Universe.

I Retain and have Access to all Memory Records of my Personal Encodements that are held within me that are required for the successful undertaking and completion of my Mission, here on Planet Earth and in this Universe.

I Retain and have Access to all the Knowledge that is held within my Sacred Heart/Mind. I AM in Constant Contact with that Knowledge.

I AM Living from within the Sacred Chambers of my Heart at all times and in all situations. I AM Free of my Past Life Incarnations.

"And So It Is!"

Prayer for the Restoration of the
Genetic Codes and DNA

I Invoke the Presence of the Elohim Council of Elders; the Co-Creator God's to be present in this now moment of time. I AM That I AM, in the image of Divine Perfection that is my Beloved Mighty I AM Presence.

I Claim my Genetic Codes and DNA to be Restored, Rejuvenated and Revivified to the New Divine Encodements of Perfection that is the Crystalline Lightbody, in accordance with the Divine Will of God, The One, the Ultimate and Supreme God of All Creations, the All That Is.

The Genetic Codes and DNA are Restored by the Elohim Council of Elders: Co-Creator God's to the Divine Perfection of the Crystalline Lightbody Encodements, for every man, woman and child on Planet Earth and throughout All the Kingdoms and Realms of Earth.

The Elohim Council of Elders and Co-Creator God's, configure the updates to the Genetic Codes and DNA Encodements that are the Crystalline Lightbody requirements for the Cosmic Ascension to the 5th Dimension and beyond, for All the Kingdoms and Realms of Planet Earth and for the Universe.

The Christed Light of God Consciousness permeates All Life Forms and All Life Force energy on Planet Earth and in the Universe, creating the Crystalline Lightbody within All Life Forms and All Life Force energy, finite and infinite.

Resurrecting in all, the Crystalline Lightbody as required for Cosmic Ascension to the 5th Dimension and Beyond. All Life Forms and All Life Force energy now have the New Encodements of the Crystalline Lightbody, elevated and Anchored, Activated, Actualized and Amplified, to be in the Awakened and Aware State of the Higher Level Consciousness of the 5th Dimension and Beyond.

God's Love Is All That Is. "And... So It Is!"

Prayer for Planetary Chakra Connection

Beloved Universal Logos: Lord Melchizedek. Galactic Logos: Lord Melchior. Solar Logos: Helios and Vesta. The Beloved Planetary Logos: Gautama Buddha. Planetary Hierarchy: Lord Sanat Kumara and Lady Venus. And the Planetary Christ, Lord Maitreya.

I AM before you now in Gratitude for my Ascension to the 5th Dimension and Beyond and I Request of you that I Be Connected to all of my Fifty Planetary Chakras in accordance with the Divine Will and Plan for my lifestream and for that which is for my Highest Good and the Highest Good of the Universe, This is in the Full Understanding that my Request of you will only occur when I AM Complete with Requirements for my Ascension to the 5th Dimension.

My Beloved Monad, my Mighty I AM Presence, upon the completion of my seven levels of initiation and in achieving the 99% light quotient level required. I Ask for my Fifty Planetary Chakras to be Installed, Activated, Actualized and Amplified, when and where appropriate.

To be fully merged with my Higher Self, my Spirit, and my Soul, with you my Beloved Mighty I AM Presence and my first nine Bodies Installed, Activated, Actualized and Amplified.

I Request that my Twelve-Strand DNA is Anchored into my Etheric Body, Activated, Actualized and Amplified. Prepare me now to be the Embodiment of and Connected with my 50 Planetary Chakras.

I AM the Embodiment of my Planetary Monad and my Mighty I AM Presence. I AM the Embodiment of my Planetary Spirit, Soul and my Higher Self. I AM the Embodiment of my Planetary Divinely Perfected Personality.

All mental, emotional and psychological issues and problems are Healed and Released. I AM the Embodiment of my Divinely Perfected

Twelve Planetary Chakras. I AM the Embodiment of my Divinely Perfected Thirteenth to Twenty Fourth Planetary Chakras available to me in the 5th Dimension and beyond. I AM the Embodiment of my Divinely Perfected Fifty Planetary Chakras Now! I AM Divinely Connected to all Fifty of my Planetary Chakras; they are completely installed to all levels of my being through my Crown Chakra. The Installation is complete for my connection to my Fifty Planetary Chakras, I AM One with my installed Fifty Planetary Chakras; they are Activated, Actualized and Amplified now, and in Divine Perfection.

I Call upon Lord Melchizedek Activate and Actualize my Fifty Planetary Chakras to Full and Complete Divine Perfection of Service to The One, the Ultimate, Supreme God of All Creation. I AM the Amplification of my complete Divinely Perfected Fifty Chakras of the Planetary System. I AM the Amplification of my Highest Potentials as gifted to me by Lord Melchizedek at my Fifty Chakras Planetary Level.

My Fifty Planetary Chakras have been installed, and Full Installation has occurred. My Fifty Planetary Chakras have been fully Activated and Actualized. My Fifty Planetary Chakras have been fully Amplified by my Planetary Ascension Lineage:

The Universal Logos: Lord Melchizedek; Solar Logos: Lord Helios and Vesta; Galactic Logos: Lord Melchior; Planetary Logos: Lord Gautama Buddha; Planetary Hierarchy: Lord Sanat Kumara and Lady Venus; Planetary Christ: Lord Maitreya; And the Planetary Teachers: Lord Serapis Bey and Master Kuthumi.

I AM in Deepest Gratitude to the Holy Spirit of the Cosmic Christed Light of God Consciousness. I AM in Humble Service to The One, the Ultimate, Supreme God of All Creation, the All That Is.

I AM that I AM, I AM All That Is!
"And... So It Is!"

Prayer and Invocation for Cosmic Protection from the Dark Forces

Beloved Elohim Council of Co-Creator God's, the Universal Hierarchy and Universal Logos, Beloved Planetary Hierarchy and Planetary Logos, Beloved Galactic Federation and the Ashtar Command, and my Beloved Mighty I AM Presence.

I Command the Protection of the Elohim Council of Elders, Co-Creator God's, the Ashtar Command, the Universal Council of Elders for All of Humanity – for Mother Earth and for the Universes, Multiverses and Omniverses from the Influence of the Dark Force Energies of Fear and Hatred.

I Command that All Dark Force Energies – whatever their form and whoever they be, that have attacked or attack, or have attached themselves or attempt to attach themselves... to destroy, harm, infiltrate in any way, shape or form any persons who are under the protection of The One, the Ultimate and Supreme God of All Creations, the Elohim: of Cosmic Christed Light of God Consciousness; and the Universal Logos: Lord Melchizedek; be removed forthwith from the Cosmic All Physicality and Metaphysically, and that their Energies be returned to the Oneness Energy of The One, the Ultimate and Supreme God of All Creations, the All That Is.

I Decree that the Galactic Federations Ashtar Command, has the authority and power to remove from Planet Earth any and all beings who threaten the well-being of those who serve The One, the Ultimate and Supreme God of All Creations, the Supreme Commander at the highest level, this pertaining to the Cosmic Ascension of Planet Earth and the Cosmic Ascension of All Humanity and all beings from All the Kingdoms and Realms of this Universe, all Multiverses and Omniverses, of this

Cosmic All, who are committed to Ascend to 5ᵗʰ Dimension and Beyond, in the taking of their Initiations and Attainments of all that which is required for their Cosmic Ascension to the Oneness of Creation.

I Command that this order is carried out immediately and that this order be for the Highest Good of All: for the Universes, Multiverses, Omniverses and Cosmic All.

In the Knowledge that it is for the Divinity of Divine Perfection in Oneness, Unconditional Love and Christed Light of God Consciousness for All beings, All Life Forms and All Life Force energy in their journey to be in Oneness of Light and Love, throughout the Cosmic Creation of The One, the Ultimate and Supreme God of All Creations, the All That Is.

"And So It Is Now!"

Prayer for World Peace

Beloved One, the Ultimate and Supreme God of All Creations, the All That Is; Beloved Cosmic Logos: the Avatar of Synthesis; the Mahatma. Universal Logos: Lord Melchizedek; Galactic Logos: Lord Melchior; Solar Logos: Helios and Vesta; The Universal Judge; Beloved Lord Sanat Kumara and Lady Venus; Lord Zohar of Shamballa; and the Spiritual Hierarchy for Planet Earth.

I Decree with all of my Sacred Heart, Spirit, Soul, Mind and Might that there be Peace on Earth and Good Will toward All Humanity through and from the Cosmic Heart, Mind and Will of God.

The Full Divine Intervention of the Godforce is now fully present to end All Wars, bringing Peace and Harmony through the Energy of the Christed Light Consciousness and Cosmic Love, Wisdom and Understanding of The One, the Ultimate and Supreme God of All Creations, to all troubled Regions of the World on Planet Earth, in this Now Moment of Time.

With All my Sacred Heart, Spirit, Soul, Mind and Might, I Affirm that God's Divine Plan of Peace and Harmony is made manifest Now! Anchored, Activated, Actualized and Amplified into All Regions of Planet Earth. I thank you and accept this as being done in accordance with the Divine Will of God, in the Divine Perfection of All That Is.

Lord, let the Golden Rain of Blessings Fall.
"And... So It Is!"

Prayer for Casting Aside the Seven Seals

Beloved One, the Ultimate and Supreme God of All Creations; Beloved Mother Earth; the Universal Logos: Lord Melchizedek. Planetary Hierarchy: Lord Sanat Kumara and Lady Venus. Planetary Logos: Lord Gautama Buddha. The Planetary Christ: Lord Maitreya. The Maha Chohan: and the Chohans of all the Twelve Sacred Flames and Rays of Christed Light of God Consciousness, and my Beloved Mighty I AM Presence.

I Affirm that you have revealed unto me the glory upon glory, power upon power, realm upon realm, until the very throne of The One, the Ultimate, Supreme God of All Creation, the All That Is has stood revealed before me.

I AM Worthy of receiving the greatest outpouring of Divine Unconditional Love and Christed Light of God Consciousness that I AM able to receive in this now moment of time. As I Stand before this wondrous Divinity of Unconditional Love and Christed Light, I AM in Boundless Thanks and Gratitude for this wondrous gift from The One, the Ultimate, and Supreme God of All Creations, the All That Is.

The Planetary Christ, Lord Maitreya, Chohan Lord Sananda and Chohan Lady Nada have Cast Aside the Seven Seals from my being that only they can remove. These Seals require the Energy of the Planetary Christed Light of God Consciousness to Release them, so that the Great Veils of Unbelief, Distrust and Separation can be Disintegrated and Dissolved. Thus, I AM Free to Receive the Divine Truth of the Eternal One.

The Seals have been removed from all parts of my Physical, Etheric, Soul and Spiritual Being, so that I AM Whole and Complete again, as per the New Encodements of Divine Perfection. These Seals have been removed from my Mind, my Heart, my Mental, Emotional and

Psychological Being, I AM Healed of the negative programs that affected my Mental and Emotional States.

I have replaced these negative programs and belief systems with the positive beliefs of the Cosmic Christed Light of God Consciousness. The Seals have been removed by the Cosmic Christed Light of God Consciousness of the Holy Spirit to Reveal the Divine Eternal Truth contained within my Spirit. My True God-Self;

I Feel Eternal Gratitude and Thank You Lord Maitreya, Lord Sananda and Lady Nada and all those who are concerned, for your wonderful Healing work and your Boundless Unconditional Love and Compassion for us All.

I LOVE YOU! "And... So It Is!"

Prayer for the Immune System

I Invoke the Energy of the Cosmic Ray for the Elemental Kingdom to Clear and Cleanse the Air, Earth and Waters of the World, of all toxic chemicals and waste matter that are affecting the Health and Well-being of Humanity and All the Kingdoms and Realms of Planet Earth extending out into the Star and Solar Systems of this Universe.

I Request that the Natural Immune System of every man, woman and child here on Planet Earth be Restored to the Divine Perfection of Optimum Perfect Health.

I Invoke the Energy of the Cosmic Love and Cosmic Light from the Source of All Life, to surround the Auric and Etheric Body of every man, woman and child, to protect the four Body System of Spirit, Soul, Mind/Emotion, Etheric and Physical Body, the Heart, Body Elemental and Inner Child from the Chemicals and Programs so designed and engineered to be detrimental to the evolving Spirit, Soul, Mind/Emotion and Physicality of Humanity.

I Request that this be done, with ease and grace and for the Highest Good of Humanity, All the Kingdoms and Realms of Planet Earth, the Universe and the Divine Mother, Mother Earth, Lady Gaia/Virgo.

"And... So It Is!"

Prayer for Breath of Integration

I Invoke the Presence of the Maha Chohan and the Chohans of the Twelve Sacred Flames and Rays to Surround me in a Circle of Sacred Fiery Light.

I Request that each of the Chohans hold in their hands the Sacred Geometric Symbol of the Sacred Flame and Ray that you represent in Christed Light of God Consciousness.

I Breathe into my entire being the frequency and vibrations that you transmit to me from these geometric symbols, with ease to aid the further integration of the Holy Spirit and Three-fold Flame within the Sacred Chambers of my Heart.

As you assist me, my entire Being is purified by your Light. I Breathe Deeply and Relax Completely into these Christed Light Energies.

I Proclaim! I AM the Resurrection and the Life of my Restored, Revitalized and Rejuvenated Crystalline Light Body, which is now energized by the Integrated Breath of Purified Light throughout my Physical Body and Body Elemental.

I AM Ready to Receive and Accept the Full Transmission of the Integrated Twelve Sacred Flames and Rays of Light Energy, at the most appropriate energy vibration levels, throughout my being to aid in the Purification, Activation, Resurrection and Restoration of the qualities of the Divine One, within me Now.

I AM in Gratitude for my Deliverance into the Divine Energies of The One, the All That Is.

I Breathe into my being the Universal Breath of The One, the Ultimate and Supreme God of All Creations, the All That Is, which are the Universal Breath of Balance and Harmony.

"And... So It Is!"

Prayer for the Departed to the Higher Realms

O Beloved Ones, as you set forth on your Journey to the Higher Realms of Cosmic Consciousness, departing the Kingdoms and Realms of Planet Earth, the Ascended Masters, the Angelic Realm, the Devic Kingdoms and the Sacred Flames and Rays of Christed Light of God Consciousness accompany you.

In Guidance, Light and Love, they surround you with the Energies of the Holy Spirit, the Godforce Energy of The One, the Ultimate and Supreme God of All Creations, the All That Is.

Beloved Ones know this well; that on your Journey Home you are Protected and Safe throughout All the Higher Realms of The One, the All That Is.

Go Forth toward the Light of Unconditional Love. See before you all the beings of Light that you know and now remember, and in Awareness you recall your Loved Ones and Friends, they are here for you to Celebrate your Journey and to Honor you and your Courage.

I, among your brethren, embrace your Journey and Thank You for being part of my Journey – the Journey of Ascension to One Unity Consciousness, Unconditional Love and the Christed Light of the Holy Spirit.

All Beings of the Cosmic Christed Light of the Holy Spirit and the Sacred Flames and Rays of Christed Light of God Consciousness surround you, to be with you on your Journey Home and support you always.

"And... So It Is!"

Prayer of Healing - Removal of All Curses

Beloved One, the Ultimate and Supreme God of All Creations; the Cosmic Hierarchy of the Elohim Council of Elders; the Universal Hierarchy and the Universal Logos: Lord Melchizedek. The Beloved Planetary Hierarchy and the Planetary Logos: Lord Gautama Buddha. The Great White Brotherhood of Light; and my Beloved Mighty I AM Presence Lord God essence of my Being;

I Command that All Negative Energies, Extra-terrestrial Negative Implants, Dark Spells and Curses that have been placed upon me (name)........................., are Removed Now, and replaced with the Divine Cosmic Light and Unconditional Love of The One, the Ultimate and Supreme God of All Creations. My Life has been resurrected to the New Encodements of Divine Perfection and Immortality, as the time for this to happen for my Highest Good and the Highest Good of the Universe is Now!

All Negative Energies, Extra-terrestrial Negative Implants, Dark Spells and Curses that had been placed upon me (name) ...., by anyone or any being, have now been removed from me and Replaced with the Divine Cosmic Light and the Unconditional Love of The One, the Ultimate and Supreme God of All Creations.

My Blueprint has been resurrected to the New Encodements of Divine Perfection and Immortality as set down by The One, the Ultimate and Supreme God of All Creations, at the beginning of my evolutionary existences. All of this has come to pass, as the time for this to happen for my Highest Good and the Highest Good of the Universe is Now!

I Command that All Dark Spells, Curses, Negative Energies, Extra-terrestrial Negative Forms and Programs that have been placed upon me (name) ...., at any time during all of my many lifetimes, across all time and space, are now removed and replaced with the Divine Perfection of The One, the Ultimate and Supreme God of All Creations.

All beings that have been responsible for casting these Black Spells, Curses and Negative Programs upon me have had their Blueprints resurrected to the New Encodements of Divine Perfection.

I AM That I AM. I Forgive all that has been done to me that bought about these Dark Spells, Negative Programs, Negative Extra-terrestrial Attachments, Implants and Curses. I Forgive myself for anything that I have done that has bought these energies into being.

"Blessed I AM, And... So It Is!"

Afterword

Blessings to each and every person who reads and uses the Prayers in this Prayer book,

I trust that your journey with these Prayers is one that Supports, Transforms and Transports you in your Cosmic Ascension – through the many higher dimensions of this Universe, the Multiverses and Omniverses beyond.

As you become more in tune with your being and in Oneness with yourself, and your Mighty I AM Presence, you thereby become more in Oneness, with Others, Humanity, the Elemental Kingdom and All the Kingdoms and Realms of this amazing Being that is Planet Earth, Our Beloved Mother, to whom we owe so much.

I ask that you take the time to Be in Gratitude and Bless our Beloved Mother Earth, for the Beauty and abundance that through her Great Love, Compassion and Wisdom, she gives to us freely.

Go forth and stand up for her in every way that you possibly can. No effort is too small in preserving her Health and Splendor. In so doing, we give thanks and appreciation for all that we receive in this now moment of time.

As WE give, so WE receive. ALL is a Reflection of our Hearts. Let our Hearts be Free, with Boundless, Unconditional Love for ALL. And the Unconditional Love is returned, Reflected unto us as Free and Boundless, Whole, Complete and in Total Oneness with The One, the Ultimate, Supreme God of All Creation – the All That Is. "And... So It Is!"

About the Author

Amerissis Kumara facilitates Spiritual Retreats in Australia and the United States of America; she is a Spiritual Healer, Teacher and Channel for the Elohim Council of Elders and the Ascended Masters.

Amerissis has a B.Msc; she is a Reiki Master Teacher Trainer, NLP Master Practitioner, Associate Accredited Certified Meta-Coach, Breathwork Practitioner and Transpersonal Counsellor, specializing in Spiritual Healing of Humanity and Planet Earth through the Sacred Flames and Rays of God Consciousness.

She has helped many people to elevate their consciousness and therefore achieve their Cosmic Ascension to the 5th Dimension and beyond in this lifetime.

Printed in the United States
By Bookmasters